T0193095

HAPPINESS:
A Choice

BARBARA A. MCLEROY

BALBOA.PRESS

A DIVISION OF HAY HOUSE

Balboa Press books may be ordered through booksellers or by contacting:

Balboa Press
A Division of Hay House
1663 Liberty Drive
Bloomington, IN 47403
www.balboapress.com
844-682-1282

Print information available on the last page.

ISBN: 978-1-9822-5963-1 (sc)
ISBN: 978-1-9822-5964-8 (e)

Library of Congress Control Number: 2020923867

Balboa Press rev. date: 12/01/2020

To Wayne, our children and spouses, and our grandchildren. You light my heart and my life with joy!

CONTENTS

PREFACE

As you read the quotes at the beginning of the first chapter of this book, you'll know if this book is for you. For some, it will be seem to be heading in a good direction. For some, it will be, to use a term my husband loved, too "airy fairy." For some, the jury may will still be out, but they'll find themselves curious and up for the adventure. There's deep trust that you'll know if this read is a stepping stone in your experience. If it is, my sincere desire is that it may be useful to you. It's the offering of my life experience that has been rich, joyous, challenging, and, oh, so educating! If it isn't your book, be encouraged in your search that the most useful tool is out there and will show up on your path. Life is all about opportunity! Endless possibilities! Choices!

We're inherently endowed at birth with the incredible gift of free will. Free will is simply the ability to choose. This book explores conscious choice in creating our experience and, hopefully, the habit of happiness. Is that even possible? Yup, it is! Is it going to be an immediate 24/7 experience? Probably not. If you look down and still see two feet firmly stationed on planet Earth, you'll remember that growth is a lifelong process, a one-choice-at-a-time process! But can happiness predominately be our experience? Absolutely. We all have the ability to choose the stories we tell in each moment. Learning to recognize those stories, or perceptions, and amending where necessary, is the key to being happy. You're in charge. Go for it!

Barbara McLeroy

ACKNOWLEDGMENTS

Support through the process of writing a book is foundational. Great appreciation goes to the clients, friends, and family who, often unknowingly, have been co-creators. For dear sister, Linda, who heard the whole thing through, thank you for your patience and your forever willingness to laugh with me at the slightest provocation! Gratitude to friends and colleagues, Mary Jo, Anne, and Joanna, who encouraged and questioned ideas along the way, allowing me to more deeply consider. For my friend and colleague, Connie, blessings and sincere appreciation for attention to the details and standing by while the many necessary decisions were made. Much love to my dear family, near and far, while often perplexed and amused by me, you are supportive beyond description and my true treasure.

The folks at Balboa Press guided this process with care and knowledge. There was never a doubt that they would light the way to completion. They made a possibly arduous process comfortably doable!

Thank you all for your part in this creation.

CHAPTER 1

The Pursuit of Happiness

The standard of success in life isn't the things. It isn't the money or the stuff—it is absolutely the amount of joy you feel.

—Abraham-Hicks

Happiness cannot be traveled to, owned, earned, worn or consumed. Happiness is the spiritual experience of living every minute with love, grace, and gratitude.

—Dennis Waitley

The one thing about which we can all probably agree is that we want to be happy. Happiness may be described differently by each us—as peacefulness, fullness, satisfaction, contentment—but we all want it. We may have different how-to formulas for achieving happiness or different ideas about what constitutes happiness, but we all desire to be happy. In fact, that desire to be happy is the driving force for every life and each action, whether or not it's recognized as such.

Wanting or desiring something is what is always moving us forward. Wanting is the hope that we'll find satisfaction, peace, and happiness in the acquisition of our current desire. Wanting, or the pursuit of happiness, is the motivation for everything that we do. Much of the time, we would be challenged to recognize that as the goal because of the silly, illogical, angry, or disrespectful behaviors we exhibit in pursuit of satisfaction. We're consistently doing what we're doing, choosing what we're choosing because, in that exact moment, we think it will get us what we want. And whatever it's that we want in any particular moment is that which we think will bring us happiness, satisfaction, contentment, and ease. Happiness is always our ultimate motivation. Let's use an imaginary situation to help us see that this is always so.

If I'm waiting to turn left at a flashing yellow arrow and you bump into the back of my car, I may choose to get out and (1) scream at you, (2) walk back and punch you, (3) become irritated and question why you would do that and what was wrong with you, (4) investigate the damage and decide what we need to do now, (5) laugh and remember the time I did that, (6) see if you're all right, (7) wave and let you know it's no problem, or (8) something else. Any action that I choose will be chosen so that I can react or respond to the situation in the way that I currently see as appropriate for dealing with it so that I may return to happiness. Granted, some options are going to be a shorter trip than others, but the goal is the same regardless of the length of the trip: I want to be happy again. The first three examples will provide the longest route for my return to happiness. The next four will be more direct. In fact, the fifth, sixth, and seventh may be demonstrations that, despite the circumstances, I never left happiness at all.

The first three constitute the long route because they assume that I have been victimized by you. Victim postures are built in delays to the pursuit of happiness. Those postures say, "I could be happy if it weren't for you and your actions. So now I'm going to have to change you, or the situation, in order to be happy." Tall order. Victim positions point to the fact that I believe my happiness is a product of what's happening in the world external to me and that it can be affected by outer circumstances. Neither of these premises is true, but they're both believed to be true by most of us.

Happiness is an internal condition repeatedly facilitated by personal choice. How we choose to view any situation is always the determiner of what follows. That choice is an expression of free will, the ability to choose. We can choose to be victims or impartial observers of what is happening in our world. That critical choice will create a life view that includes or excludes happiness. If we choose to be at the mercy of worldly circumstances, we'll feel victimized and powerless because we'll be unable to control the circumstances that we think will make us happy. If we believe happiness is dependent on copacetic externals, when things are smooth in our world, we'll be temporarily happy, but the unpredictable looms around the corner. When things do get bumpy again, we'll be distressed, fearful, and once more feel helplessly at the whim of external situations.

Contrastingly, if we behave as one-step-back or impartial observers of our world, we're able to choose how we interpret its events. We don't assume that our happiness is disturbed when something occurs that isn't what we expected or wanted. We watch and remain open to what is happening without judgment about it. We can choose to be balanced and maintain our peace despite the circumstances. When we're willing to observe instead of instantly reacting to changes in the world, happiness isn't discarded because circumstances shift. Circumstances will always shift. We must learn to watch them do so with equanimity, not rushing to interpretation but allowing the meaning of the situation to emerge. As the events of life continue to change, only from the perspective of impartial observer will we have access to the choice of its interpretation. If we fail to perceive this access to choice, we'll automatically react to the changing circumstances of life with fear. Fight or flight is the practiced way to deal with fear. For the protection of the body, those are appropriate options. However, when the body is safe, we often still use these responses. When the body is safe, it's the perceived loss of external control that fuels our reaction. Fear is the habit of lifetimes, predicated on the mistaken belief that we can control the momentary, shifting external world and circumstances. We cannot.

As we're learning to intentionally choose happiness, there will be those times when we're unwilling to choose it. Instead, we'll assume the habitual perspective of fear and consequent victimization. Because we're becoming aware that choice resides within us, it's only a matter of time until we'll consistently become aware and access that power to choose. Once we understand that true power is the power of choice, we can never again be blindly controlled by the world's circumstances or perceive ourselves as victims of it.

Let's illustrate this idea. If I believe you've done something to me, my perception creates a separation between us. Separation is a you-versus-me perspective. You're the bad guy, and I'm the wronged one, the innocent one. If I decide you're the "bad guy," I've attacked you with my judgment about you. There is no way we can get to the peace or happiness we would prefer from a choice to attack or oppose each other. Oppositional postures create separation. It isn't possible to gain any measure of happiness when we're separate or opposed to each other. Being "right" becomes more important than being happy.

Victimization is always the choice to be separate or opposed. And as we'll come to understand, it doesn't matter whether we're the victim or the victimizer—both aspects keep us apart, separated. Interestingly, we play both roles at the same time. When we perceive ourselves as victimized, as attacked, we chose that fearful perception. Because we made that choice, we automatically choose something/someone outside of us as responsible for the attack. Hence, we're the victimizer by that choice to blame. In the choice for victimization, we may get to be "right," but we'll never be truly happy. Happiness cannot be found in attack and separation.

On the other hand, when I simply observe what has happened and refrain from putting a premature meaning to it. I simply realize, or accept, the situation as it is: a happening. From this perspective, I'm in an open place to explore it with you. I might as well accept it because in is over and has happened. This does not mean that I like it, want it, or do not wish to do something in response. It simply means that I see what has occurred.

About now, you're probably saying, "Well, that might be possible to do in this made up situation that is pretty minor, but what about the more critical situations?" Actually the same concept, or truth applies. No matter what the situation, we always have the choice to accept it in the moment and then decide what is next. While we may prefer that the situation be different, the only logical thing to do is accept it as it is because that is how it is in this moment. No amount of raging, weeping, gnashing, or lamenting will change what we think *is* because it's actually what *was*. Do you get that? As soon as we have noticed anything, it has already happened—it's over. We speak of it as what is, but actually it's what *was* by the time we notice it. Clearly, we know that what was is over, is now in the past, and there is absolutely nothing that changes the past. It's done. It's over. It's in the past. It's unalterable. All that can be done is to decide what's next in response to what was.

When we understand that simple concept, we save ourselves so much frustration, anger, and grief. Often, instead of accepting what has occurred, we spend enormous time and energy resisting the obvious. We can't believe this is happening to us. We're furious that we should have to put up with this. We won't accept this; we absolutely will not accept this! In these ways and a myriad of others, we resist our experiences. We want the past changed! Impossible. Peace requires that we accept what has occurred rather than resist it. Our various postures of resistance don't alter the experiences one wit and actually serve to prolong the discomfort associated with them.

Our resistance and denial keep us from moving forward into the only process that can create difference and allow us to escape from our discomfort, that is, moving to decision about what is next. Until we're ready to move forward, we'll be stuck in what we don't want for as long as we care to be. Isn't it amazing that we don't recognize what we're doing at the time? Isn't it astounding that we willingly compound the perception of the problem rather than be willing to move to the solution? The movement toward solution, or the answer, is always the beginning of the return to peace and happiness. Do you suppose that it's possible to be so good at accepting what is, that problematic, victimization viewpoints could eventually fade from our experience? Oh happy day! Literally.

If this is resonating with you in any way, you're well on your way to creating the consistent happiness you want in your life. Until we recognize our own responsibility as the creators of our problematic views, or our accepting views, we're powerless to truly affect our own happiness. Once we realize and take responsibility for the choice of view (perception, story), and see how it impacts every situation, we're well on our way to claiming the true power given us in our creation: the power of free will or free choice. This is *huge*. How we choose to view something is the most determining factor in our experience of it. We're continually imprisoned or freed, upset or happy, by our chosen points of view. Amazing, isn't it? We're powerful creators and made so by the ability to choose our perceptual perspective. We're always doing that anyhow. Why not do it intentionally?

Summary of Key Ideas

- We all want to be happy. All behaviors are motivated by that desire.
- Happiness is an internal condition repeatedly facilitated by personal choice.
- How we choose to view something is the most determinative factor in our experience of it. All meaning comes from us.
- We're fearful when we believe we're at the mercy of external circumstances.
- Fear is the belief that externals, and control of externals, govern happiness.
- Only as observers of our world will we have access to the choice for interpreting its events.
- "What is" is actually "what was" by the time we notice it. It's in the past.
- Nothing changes the past.
- Resistance to current circumstances prolongs and delays happiness.
- Peace requires we accept what has happened rather than resist it.
- Then choose what's next.
- Discomfort signals the need for a change in perception.
- Because we choose our perceptions, we act in response to our own perception.
- Free will, this ability to choose, is inherently a part of being human.

CHAPTER 2

The Only Real Choice

Man is born as a seed; it all depends on you, what you do with yourself; it all depends on whether you grow or you don't. It is your choice— and each moment the choice has to be faced; each moment you are on the crossroads.

—Osho

Positive and negative emotions cannot occupy the mind at the same time.

—Napoleon Hill

Once you understand that the only meaning anything has is the meaning you give it, you will begin to move beyond the requirements of history to reinforce itself upon the present moment and then dictate the future in agreement to what was. … How you perceive anything is a direct action of the consciousness you hold.

—The Guides through Paul Selig

You have garnered, by now, that there are really only two choices for perceiving all the situations of our lives: the choice for victimization or the choice for freedom. The two choices could be called the self-serving ego (little self, me first) or the aligned (true self, us) view. Said in another way, it's the choice for fear, guilt and separation or the choice for happiness, joining, and love. We truly want only one of these.

As we have already said, victimization is a viewpoint that creates separation. In victimization, we become resistant to each other; we're against each other, both fighting for the superior or "right" position. We manipulate each other to achieve this position, feel guilty inside for doing so, and then are fearful as we wait for retribution. We may see this retribution as coming from the other party or from "God" as punishment for our ugly behavior.

Manipulative behaviors are always ugly by their very nature. We use manipulation to make someone feel guilty so that they will do what we want them to do, and then feel guilty ourselves, acknowledged or not, for doing so. We manipulate most frequently with anger. Anger is the little dance we do that demonstrates how awful you (they) are for what you (they) did to me. It's a drama to coerce you (them) into behaving how I want you to behave. It's definitely a victim posture and motivated by the fear of not having control.

I remember a situation not too long ago when I was driving my grandson back to his home. We were returning at a busy time of day, and as I began to turn left onto the expressway ramp, I heard the squealing of brakes and saw a car that I had failed to see come to a screeching halt before me. I stopped in time, and we didn't hit, but it was more to his good driving than mine. This man was clearly furious with me and pulled his car forward onto the ramp and turned it sideways to block traffic. He got out and came stomping back toward me. For some fortuitous reason, perhaps because my grandson was keenly watching from the back seat, I remained calm and rolled down my window. This man began yelling and screaming at me (I don't need to write the words), and I quietly agreed with everything he said. He was correct in his assessment (though quite disrespectful in the delivery). I had been careless. I wasn't driving well. I had made a mistake. I earnestly apologized. I was very regretful for this error. And I was relatively unaffected by the tirade. I was calm and sincerely apologetic. This was not satisfying, in any way, to this person. In livid frustration, he turned around, marched back to his car, and squealed away onto the expressway. I regretted later that I hadn't had the presence of mind to appreciate him for his skillful driving. My grandson and I had a wonderful conversation about the futility and danger of anger. I was so grateful that I, too, didn't choose to be victimized by his tirade, disrespect, and angered at the situation. What "was" is over, and the only sane behavior was choosing the quickest route back to happiness. I hoped that his driving home would not be adversely affected by his chosen fury at me. Of course, it was motivated by the fear of the near collision. We reacted to that fear differently.

His anger was an attempt to coerce me to somehow change what I had done in the past. I knew that couldn't be done. His choice to be a victim of me was also the choice, justified in his mind, to be the victimizer of me. As stated earlier, when we're victimized by anyone or anything, we must select the "reason." Thus, we become victimizers ourselves. These reciprocal aspects of victimization are always present together and are the process of choosing to be manipulated and to manipulate by guilt. It's easily seen that guilt is only used for separation and therefore cannot ever get us that which we most desire: happiness. Happiness is always and only produced through joining. In the above situation, my willingness to join could only be met if he chose to abandon his victim posture. Had that occurred, we could have transitioned from great fearful separation to grateful joining, an immediate healing of the circumstances and perhaps gratitude for our safety. When "right" is more important, joining isn't the priority. When we choose to be "right," we automatically exclude the opportunity to be happy, peaceful, easy.

When we choose to be right, it implies that someone must be wrong. Right always includes the polarity of wrong—a separation has been perceived. Right automatically creates a hierarchy with the "right person" being higher up the ladder than the "not-right person." The right person "wins" at the expense of the "wrong" person. Happiness cannot be found in these dynamics.

It seems important to add to the driving scenario that my work was to continue to *not* see myself as victimized by him. My ego was tempted to feel beat up. My task was to simply see it as a happening, to be grateful that we were all safe and that I had a chance to practice peace. While I didn't enjoy such an angry, crass, vehement outburst, I realized that, in his fear, he was doing the best he knew how to address it. I would like to think that he continued to think about our interchange and hoped that he would choose to behave differently in his future upsets. If I had counterattacked him, that possibility wouldn't exist because it would have fueled his justification for behaving as he had. My hope was that he would eventually be able to accept my sincere apology and use it all as learning. I certainly did.

This story illustrates a very challenging aspect of the work we're all doing, as we grow in healing our tendency for victim postures. It's a tendency that is alive and well in all of us. It's a growth point of the human condition. There is a line in *A Course in Miracles* that says, "Beware of the temptation to perceive yourself unfairly treated." We're so easily tempted to believe we've been mistreated. Healing our willingness to see ourselves as victimized is an enormous aspect of personal growth. It's a lesson we're all learning; only the circumstances are different. At one time or another, we all succumb to believing we're being mistreated. Do you realize it's impossible to be mistreated without our own perception of mistreatment? We can never be victimized without our own participation. We participate by believing it's so! Let me offer an absurd example that I often use to make the point:

I'm sitting in my office working with a client and a hypothetical stranger opens the door and yells at me, "You're the dumbest woman on the planet!" As I hear those words, I have a critical choice to make: Do I know or not know the meaning of this situation? If I do know the meaning: "This person has no right to interrupt me when I'm working," "It's rude to burst in here in this manner," "Someone is attacking me," "No one ever respects my personal space," "Someone has escaped from an institution," and so on, I'm going to feel mistreated, belittled, offended, attacked and will respond as being victimized. That usually means I will counter attack in some manner. I will go out in the hall and (1) ask, "Who do you think you are?" (2) grab him by the shirt and threaten to hit him, (3) call the police, (4) start crying and wonder why everything happens to me, (5) or some other counterproductive behavior. I will keep the separation going with my defensive response. I'm innocent and have been injured and you're the perpetrator, the bad one. I'm entitled to recompense and you're responsible. Victim, victim, victim.

If I don't know the meaning of this situation, I'm open to an entirely different set of responses. I may look at the door and say, (1) "Pardon?" (2) "Please don't come in uninvited," (3) "I'm not sure I understand," (4) "I'm busy right now, but if you will sit on the porch a moment, let's talk about this when I'm finished," (5) "I hear your opinion. Would you please close the door?" (6) [laughingly say] "Some days it feels like that. Please leave and close the door," (7) or another statement to defuse the situation. I allow him his opinion and don't assume it's about me in any way—because it isn't! In order to believe I'm mistreated, I have to perceive the idea of mistreatment. When I don't know what the situation means, there's no automatic perception of mistreatment. Refraining from judgmentally knowing the meaning of a situation creates the space for the deeper, true meaning to emerge.

In this absurd situation, I don't know why this person is behaving like this, but it isn't about me. I may have to deal with the situation, but I'm not personally affronted. Just like the previous traffic incident, I haven't perceived myself as unfairly treated. While I may have preferred that the situation hadn't occurred, I haven't been attacked by it, and the logical thing to do is whatever is appropriately next. Even if that means ushering the person out of the building, calling the police to remove the person, or just locking my door, I don't have to do it from the perspective of having been persecuted. I simply do it, because that's what I've decided is next. It's my mental attitude that makes all the difference. Am I mentally separating or joining? I can call the police from a place of joining because I think this is the best action in the interest of this person, my client, and myself. It's never the behavior that makes the distinction between separation and joining, but the motivation for the behavior. Our every action is motivated by the desire to separate or join, by fear or love, by guilt or happiness—different descriptors, same idea.

Look again at that statement from *A Course in Miracles*, "Beware of the temptation to perceive yourself unfairly treated." Isn't that word *temptation* an interesting choice? Why would we possibly be tempted to perceive mistreatment? There must be some payoff, some gain for us to want to choose a perception of being mistreated. That's exactly so. Every victim posture identifies with a specialness of being deserving. Deserving of what is specific to the victim. Every time we choose to perceive ourselves as victimized, we automatically believe we're entitled to recompense. They have done it to us, and now they must pay up! We love to live from this place of entitlement! That is the seduction of victimization—others will be responsible for our well-being, not us. In truth, that is, of course, not the case and never will be. Thankfully, we have the responsibility of our own well-beings and the power to create it through the choice of perception.

Summary of Key Ideas

- There are only two choices for perceiving all circumstances: love or fear, victimization or freedom, joining or separation. These characterize the same choices.
- Victimization is an attacking viewpoint that creates separation and guilt. It assumes entitlement and fears retribution.
- Victimization is a manipulation. Manipulation is used to get what we want—without directly asking!
- The choice to be a victim of someone or something requires we select the victimizer thus becoming the victimizer ourselves through that selection. Victim/victimizer always coexist.
- Guilt always creates separation. It's never the behavior that makes the distinction between separation and joining but the motivation for the behavior.
- When I choose to be "right," I separate and exclude the opportunity to be happy.
- Happiness is produced through joining.
- Beware of the temptation to perceive yourself unfairly treated. (*A Course In Miracles*)
- It's impossible to be mistreated without our own perception of mistreatment.
- Healing victimization is an enormous aspect of personal growth. We can never be victimized without our own participation.
- Refraining from judgmentally knowing the meaning of a situation, allows the deeper, true meaning to emerge.
- We have the responsibility for our own well-being and the power to create it through our choice of perception.

CHAPTER 3

Growing Beyond Victimization

Whether you think you can, or you think you can't—
you're right.

— Henry Ford

It takes half your life before you discover life is a do-it-
yourself project.

—Napoleon Hill

If we truly desire happiness, growing beyond, or healing victim consciousness, seems to be a necessary step for the human experience. We all choose self-serving victim postures as attempts to level the playing field in our maturation process. We learn this as children when we feel powerless with our more powerful parents. Obvious demonstrations of our childlike victim consciousness behaviors are temper tantrums, whining, screaming, outrageous crying, pouting, and so on. If these become useful in gaining what we want, we'll continue to use them as manipulative power-gaining tools into adulthood. James Redfield, in his book, *The Celestine Prophesy,* refers to these tools as control dramas and categorizes them as intimidation, interrogation, aloof, and poor-me. Control dramas will be individually discussed further in the following chapter.

All of these control dramas characterize victimization attempts to gain the upper hand (power) when we're fearful of loss of control (powerless). By their very nature, victim postures are manipulative. They lack the integrity of simply asking for what we want, accepting the response and maturely deciding what to do next. Victim postures are the tools of the constantly fearful ego.

They are the fearful part of us that believes we're here on our own and unsupported. That part of us is always out to "get" and to prove its worthiness and superiority. We call it the self-serving ego. The ego needs to be the winner—always, and often at the expense of others. To the ego, defeat isn't seen as part of the learning process but a proof of inferiority that it doesn't tolerate lightly.

To restate it simply, a victim posture is when we place the circumstances or others as who or what is responsible for our well-being or happiness. It puts that responsibility as dependent on externals, those things outside of us. That is never an accurate perception, but it takes a level of maturation and personal responsibility to understand this. When we're young, we think life is controlled by external people and events. Those things happening to us and those situations create our happiness or unhappiness. In truth, these events and situations are simply the catalysts for our personal perceptions or stories about them—to which we respond. In victimization, we believe the event is causal. In actuality, it's our perception of the event, or story about the event, that is the causal element. Always. Nothing can happen to us without our thinking it so.

Example:

> A woman has decided to make tacos for dinner. She has started the meal and goes to get the taco seasoning. When she goes to her spice cabinet, she discovers there is no taco seasoning. This is the choice point that determines her happiness—for which she is always in charge! If she becomes

angry, frustrated, upset in any way, she is allowing
the circumstance to control her happiness. She is
a victim of no seasoning—by her own choice of
perspective. She blames her husband, who did
the shopping. She blames herself for forgetting
to put it on the list. She blames her neighbor for
borrowing it. She blames her husband for cooking
tacos last time and not telling her he used it all—
whatever. She negatively projects responsibility
and she is unhappy.

Conversely, she accepts that there is no taco
seasoning, for whatever reason, and decides
what to do next. This is the most expedient and
peaceful way to proceed. At some point, we
proceed anyway, so let's skip the victim drama.
She may decide to look up a tacos seasoning
recipe and make her own from the spices on hand.
She may call her neighbor and borrow some. She
may make a quick switch to spaghetti sauce. She
may run to the store. She may decide it's dinner
out tonight. In other words, she accepts what is
and doesn't let the external circumstance absorb
her happiness, she just accepts what is and decides
how to proceed.

In both options above, it's a choice as to whether it's a big deal
or not. How the situation was viewed determined what followed.
As previously described, this is always how it works. We're the
determiners of our happiness, our comfort, or our unhappiness,
our discomfort, by the stories we tell in response to everything.
This story, or perception, usually isn't verbal. It's an automatic
mental process that happens in less than a second. It also has a
vibrational component that we'll look at later. We're the observers
of our lives and the interpreters of their meaning.

19

Again, all meaning comes from us! Something is observed, and we rush into our past experience to understand the event. Then we project that meaning onto the event and believe that is the reality of it. There is no intrinsic reality. It's all projected by us! *There is no objective reality*—it's all subjective. Understanding this dynamic makes us completely in charge of our own happiness. We're the one telling the story—always. Uncomfortable feelings are a signal that we don't like the story we're telling. Discomfort is the obvious clue that change is needed. The needed change is about our story, the internal interpretation that we have projected onto the situation and believed real. If the feelings resulting from our story, or projection, are any form of discomfort, the current projection doesn't serve us.

By learning to simply accept events and decide what's next, we spend less time with discomforting projections and just get on with what to do now. We're always the chooser in how to proceed, whether we take responsibility for the choice or blame it on someone or some circumstance (victimization). Observing and accepting what's before us is the most expedient and comfortable process.

When we allow ourselves to be derailed by a circumstance or person(s), our misperceptions are always the causal factor. In victimization, we project all responsibility beyond ourselves onto the external factors. Until we recognize our roles in projection, we'll continue to do this. We always have the choice to realign with peace. If we believe we have no role in its creations, we'll continue to see ourselves at the whim of external circumstances and people. Sometimes, we're sufficiently distanced from our ability to choose, that it takes a while to remember we have it. We always have it. It's the free will with which we were endowed at birth.

If we have developed the habits of victimization, blaming externals, we may forget we have choice and live, for a while, from victim posturing. Some live whole lives from this perspective. We all know people who are frequently angry or irritable, complain a lot, reject all responsibility for the stories they tell, and truly believe things could be different if it weren't for something or someone else. We know people who feel they have been dealt unfair hands, people who feel overwhelmed by life. We know bullies, tyrants, boasters, and those who are timid and unconfident. These are all victim postures, and we have probably worn some of those characterizations at one time or another in our own growth processes. It's important to understand victimization, be aware of our own habits, and learn to come from a place of more integrity and responsibility.

Yes, integrity. As previously shown, victim postures are lacking integrity because they are manipulative. They are a dishonest, veiled attempts to get someone else to do something so that we can be happy again. But often, we don't let them know what we want outright because of our fear that they won't give it to us. We want someone else to make our life better, to be responsible for our happiness. It's an inside job. We're truly the only ones responsible for our happiness. Our own perception is just that, our own. We can pretend "they made me do it," but it just isn't so. They can't choose *our* perceptions. If they could, they would probably choose one that made us happy!

How do we unwittingly keep this victim posture operating in our lives? We may have learned this dynamic in our families, in the workplace, in the educational process. We may have had a traumatic circumstance that overwhelmed us and made us feel rudderless. Whatever the reason, we're fearful and attempting to control the externals so *whatever* won't continue or ever happen again. We push against the externals to try and gain internal ground.

There are some tell-tale victim behaviors that can alert us to these manipulative postures. First, in most cases, as victims we'll try to "sell" the position. Through verbal and nonverbal expression, we want to make others aware of what we perceived as "not right." We want others to agree to and join our misperception to help it gain ground and to be right! The ego glories in "right." This is what displays of temper, withdrawal, dominance, whining, poor me stories are actually trying to accomplish—to form a posse for being right! We feel justified in our positions when we can get others to help validate them. What we don't recognize, in doing this, is that others will naturally resist the "sell." They subconsciously feel the manipulative nature of this behavior. Resistance to this manipulation will be demonstrated in their trying to offer solutions, get away as soon as they are able, placating, and so on. And, interestingly, victims will always defend their position by rejecting help, by telling us why our solution won't work. How could they/we remain victims if a solution is allowed? Nuts, right? We all do it!

Let's be clear. Victim postures are subversive power grabs. In victimization, we're fearful of loss of control and desperate to regain it. Fear is the motivator always. From our own perception, we feel powerless and desperate for support. Selling the victim story, our misperception, is a veiled attack in an attempt to gain the love and the joining with others from which we have disconnected. We feel separate, alone, and in varying degrees of discomfort or desperation. Victim postures are very misguided attempts to heal our feelings of separation, and they manipulate others into a false sort of joining. There is no lasting happiness to be found through victimization.

Anger is an escalated attempt to sell a victim posture. In truth, it's simply a distracting smokescreen to hide fear. It's a manipulative attempt to get others to comfort us and address/support our fears. Anger is always a victim posture. When we're absorbed in our angry dance, all attention is on keeping it going. We believe it will convince others to support us by joining the dance. Anger is a manipulative sell that attempts to draw others into our drama and gather a posse supporting our view.

With anger, as soon as I can become aware of my current war dance, I can step off the drama stage and into the audience as an observer. This is where the choice for change becomes possible. Knowing anger is a victim posture and, therefore, manipulative, I'm aware I want to have more integrity in my interactions. I must face myself and ask these questions: What do I want in this moment? Am I willing to straightforwardly ask for what I want?

Holding onto anger is like drinking poison and expecting the other person to die.

—The Buddha

At our best, when we're confronted with victim behaviors in others, we can recognize them for what they are and bypass the drama of the incident being reported and find a way to stand by, to truly join. We understand the victim perspective is motivated by fear. We support the person, and don't buy the perceptual drama being offered. We can't fix anyone else's story. We can always offer support while they find their way. When we truly want to support another who is lost in victim, we might silently ask ourselves, "What would love, kindness, and compassion do now?" This keeps our focus out of the drama and truly with the one clearly calling for support. There is a beautiful line from *A Course in Miracles*, which, paraphrased, states, "Everything is either the extension of love or the call for it. Our responsibility is the same either way." We meet both with love, kindness, and compassion.

As we desire to support the person, not the drama, we may say, "Gosh, sounds very confusing (difficult, overwhelming, challenging, etc.)." We might suggest a little time out with a nap, or lunch, or a walk in the park. We may not say anything but pat a shoulder, listen attentively, or give short syllables to indicate our attention—"Mmmm," "Oh," "Yeah." There is no prescription other than genuine caring, however that seems appropriate. We didn't create this problem, and we can't fix it. The person with the problem is the person with the problem. It's always a problem of misperception. Only the perceiver can make the correction. Our role is support only.

When we become skilled in recognizing victim postures, we'll recognize our own more quickly and understand our roles in creating them through the choices of perception. We'll be willing to admit misperception and ask Inner Wisdom, Source Energy, Higher Power, or whatever to helps us see differently, to correct the misperception. That help is always given. Guaranteed. It's the nature of the Energy that creates and continues to sustain us. We can choose whether or not to avail ourselves of it. It's there either way.

As we become committed to healing our victim perspectives, we may think *we* can correct our own misperceptions. That is ego arrogance and looks like going into the closet and switching our black hat for a white one. Looking better isn't the solution. We just don't have the needed perspective. If we did, we would have already applied it! We must elicit the help of True Wisdom. That is why we ask to see differently. Again, the simple question "What would love do now?" also creates connection with True Wisdom. Each sincere seeker finds the asking process that works for them.

One spiritual teaching says, "Ask and it shall be given to you. Seek and you shall find" (Holy Bible, Matthew 7:6).

So healing the perception of victimization is part of the process of every life. Again, if we look down and have two feet in the experience of planet Earth, this healing is on the learning agenda. Belief systems are composed of collections of perceptions—or misperceptions. Our happiness indicates which way we're currently leaning. The sooner and more regularly we recognize and address the misperceptions, the happier we'll be. It's the life work of creating our own happiness.

Summary of Key Ideas

- Situations are simply catalysts for our personal perceptions or stories about them. Belief systems are composed of collections of perceptions.

- In victimization, we believe the event is causal. In actuality, it's our perception of the event, or story about the event projected onto it, which is the causal element.

- When we refuse victim perspectives, we step off the battlefield. We reject separation and the dis-empowering idea of you against me. Unwilling "to perceive ourselves unfairly treated," we have no need for defense or counterattack.

- Growing beyond and healing victim consciousness seems to be a necessary step for the human experience if we desire true happiness.

- By learning to simply accept events and decide what's next, we spend less time with discomforting projections and just get on with what to do now.

- Discomfort signals our current perception doesn't serve us.

- We're the observers of our life and the interpreters of its meaning. All meaning comes from us!

- There is no intrinsic, objective reality. It's all subjective, projected—by us.

- We're the determiner of our happiness or unhappiness by the story we tell in response to everything.

- Uncomfortable feelings are a signal that we don't like the story we're telling. They signal that change of perception is needed.

- Life situations are the catalysts for our growth, onto which we project meaning.

- We can accept what is and not let the external circumstance absorb our happiness. We accept what is, then we decide how to proceed.

CHAPTER 4

Control Dramas

Everyone manipulates for energy either aggressively, directly forcing people to pay attention to them, or passively, playing on people's sympathy or curiosity to gain attention.

—James Redfield, *The Celestine Prophecy*

When we're young, we develop strategies to even the playing field when we feel overpowered by our parents. In other words, we develop unconscious strategies to get our way! These strategies are sometimes called control dramas. They are always an ego manipulative attempt to be more powerful than we currently feel. When we fear simply asking for what we want, or having asked and been denied, we up the ante using a control drama. Whining and temper tantrums are the most obvious. We all can probably tell a story similar to the one that follows.

As a young child, shopping with my mother was an activity I enjoyed, and my younger brother did not. As a two-year-old (I was five), he would simply lie down on the store floor and hold his breath when he didn't want to shop any more. This became routine and an effective, intimidating strategy that would curtail shopping or have mother negotiating promises of brevity. One day, with trepidation and great courage, Mama and I decided to walk away. Of course, this appeared awful to onlookers. But as hoped, he breathed, got up, and quickly ran to catch up. Being a quick study, when he learned holding his breath no longer worked, he developed a new method, which was to simply run away! When we feel powerless to manage the external situation, we employ manipulative techniques to grab power back.

Control dramas are one way to characterize these manipulative techniques. James Redfield, in *The Celestine Prophecy*, classifies the four control dramas as *intimidation, interrogation, aloof,* and *poor me*.

We usually develop a "speciality," but we can actually use any of them when we deem it necessary to gain the ever-allusive physical control. We develop our own particular control dramas in response to the ones used most commonly in our experience.

Intimidation

As the word implies, intimidation is an attempt to make another feel powerless by our perceived dominance. We feel threatened in the presence of intimidation. It may be so subtle that we don't even understand it. My dad used intimidation. When in high school, a boy I was dating commented in the car, after picking me up, "I'd like it if you could be ready when I come to pick you up. Your dad never talks when I wait in the living room with him. It's weird." That was just dad. He didn't talk if he didn't want to talk. We were used to it; my date wasn't. It felt uncomfortable, intimidating to him. Dad is long passed, so I can't ask him if it was intentional. Knowing Dad—probably. I was the first born, and it was most likely a behave-yourself message to my date.

Scapegoating can be another form of intimidation. It's an irresponsible, often bullying attempt to make someone else the reason for our unhappiness or discomfort. Of course, it's always our own misperceptions of the situation which are the stimuli for our upsets. Remember: all control dramas are various victim postures—costumes, you might say, in our attempt to cast blame so we can be the powerful one. Control dramas are always motivated by fearing loss of control.

Anger is an obvious form of intimidation. It's a dramatic grab for control. The bigger the anger dance, the more we're distracted from the dancer's underlying fear of loss of control. The implication being broadcast by the anger dance is that you're responsible for my upset! We now know that just can't be so.

Interrogation

Interrogation, as the word suggests, asks questions in an attempt to judge another as lacking or wrong, so that one may feel superior. Sometimes this is very subtle and guised as interest. It isn't genuine interest but feigned interest with a design to grab power by being better, wiser, stronger, and so on. Mama used interrogation. I remember that often when I came home from a date, she would ask what seemed like a million questions about where I had been and what I'd done. She questioned until she could find a place of disappointment, disapproval, or correction. I now understand her fear for my safety, which motivated this behavior. Then it was just annoying and facilitated the creation of my own control drama: aloof. I learned that little provided information yielded little criticism. Mama had grown up with a very confident, intimidating mother and never quite developed her own deep confidence. That reticence and sense of insufficiency prompted her fears and her need to be overly fearful for her children.

Sometimes when we want someone to do something for us, we fear that direct, up-front asking may not deliver the result we want. So we develop leading questions hoping to guide the direction. When another asks me, "What are you doing Thursday afternoon?" I see where this is going and get directly to the point, "What do you want me to do?" This question moves the discussion out of interrogating manipulation to honest exchange.

Aloof

As said before, aloof is my specialty. I would like to say *was* my specialty, but it still threatens to come into play in some situations. I'm very much alert to its character and, hopefully, find my way back to honesty as soon as possible. Aloof is characterized by withdrawal and false reservedness. We "aloofs" pull back in an effort to gain power by making the other person come after us. A classic aloof exchange might be as follows: To the aloof: "What's the matter with you?" The aloof characteristically replies, "Oh nothing." Clearly, it's something! And the power tug of war ensues.

Let's not confuse this with genuine withdrawal, where wisdom prevails when it seems there can be no beneficial movement at the present moment and it's recognized that a time-out is genuinely needed. Recognizing the need for a pause allows us to breathe and to rebalance before proceeding.

A funny aside about genuine time-outs, sent to me from my friend who is Gramma to Evie (age, four):

"Evie just told me I needed to get a basement in case she needed a time-out. I told her I could use the garage. Her response: 'No thanks.'" Loved Evie's honesty! Genuine time-outs are honest; aloof withdrawals are not.

The aloof is the subtlest of the control dramas. While all control dramas have manipulative hidden agendas, the aloof is the most elusive. Because of this added lack of transparency, aloof may remain off in their withdrawn, falsely superior perspective if the other involved doesn't pursue them. They withdraw into their victim posture. Young children often don't do this as quietly. I remember a young grandchild who, having petulantly withdrawn rather than comply, started throwing the shoes that were closely available. Aloofs want to be pursued! How can they maintain their manipulative power otherwise? This stubborn child, like my brother earlier, had clearly upped the ante!

Poor Me

This is probably the most obvious of the control dramas when we're alert. It's a clear demonstration and announcement of victim posturing. This drama clearly projects all responsibility for what is happening beyond themselves in very overt ways. The poor-me drama, like all control dramas, holds something or someone else to blame for the perceived misfortune they're now facing. Their perception puts others obviously responsible for their lack of happiness.

In young children, we see this as demonstrated by whining, crying, and angry outbursts when things don't go their way. They want you to see how unhappy *you* have made them. This is the frustration of the young when they feel powerless to match parental control. I remember the attempt of a young child in our family, my sister, who once complained, "See what you made me did!" Clearly, the child wasn't responsible! In more intentionally humorous ways, that phrase became a favorite of all of us in the years that followed.

Interestingly, we're often "hooked" by the poor-me drama. If we don't recognize the dynamics, we may genuinely offer logical solutions for the perceived problem. This will be where we can gain our first insight to what is going on. Guaranteed, a person who is stuck in a poor-me victim posture will not accept help. Victims will argue for their limitations. How could they maintain their misperceived advantage if they gave it up? They would no longer be manipulating to get something they wanted and gain the elusive ego control, if they allowed their perceived problem to be solved.

We all have known and may have, at times, been people whose perspective is always about what is currently lacking in their life. We're always going to hear something about what is "wrong" now. If we're honest with ourselves, we have probably developed an aversion to being with these people and don't fully

31

know why. It's the uncomfortable manipulative nature of the victim posture that repels us. The poor me is always openly selling their current upset. When we get "hooked," we'll think it wouldn't be kind to withhold help.

As suggested earlier, real help in these situations is supporting the person but not their misperception. We can't fix another's problem. It's their misperception that created it. But we can certainly support them while they do their work. We're most helpful when we can keep our own ego out of the mix by not demonstrating our superior knowing of what the solution might be. How could we know? Trust me: our all-knowing ego will definitely want to tell them how to fix this and get on with it! This is never true help. Instead, we leave the problem with them simply because it isn't ours. I often remind myself, "The person with the problem is the person with the problem!" We don't help ourselves or others, if we assume their misperceptions.

To be truly helpful, we might say, "Gosh, that really seems difficult. What are you thinking about doing?" Or, simply, "I can see how upsetting this is." Or if you're truly willing, "May I help in any way?" As discussed earlier, our role is to support the other in their own choice process, not to make the choice. We naturally do this with children as we help them become responsible and develop their own skills. They know they have us as backup support, as encouragers for their decision making. We're willing to help brainstorm, but the choice of direction is theirs. It's most difficult if we see a bit of harsh learning in the consequences that will likely follow for the direction they're choosing.

Discerning between poor me and genuine asking for help is important. We have all been with another in overwhelming situations. They may even temporarily feel victimized, but they don't wish to remain there. Help is appreciated and considered in these circumstances. We all have been so overwhelmed that we truly couldn't think rationally. We can help by holding the space, or making a needed decision, until the other can reestablish some kind of equilibrium. Our offer of a meal, a ride, a hug, or any sincere supportive measure will be accepted. We help the other find their way back to balance, from which rational decision making can be again accessed. We have all offered this kind of support when someone we care about experiences significant loss. There is no victim manipulation going on in these circumstances, even though the person suffering may *temporarily* feel victimized by it. We're overwhelmed by life on occasion. Willingness to regroup and move ahead characterizes rebalance at these times.

To recap, the four controls dramas are dishonest and manipulative forms of seeking to grab power in subversive ways. They are separating behaviors and always seek gain at the expense of someone else's well-being. Control dramas can never generate the harmonious joining we all desire in our relationships. It takes courage to look at our own manipulative ego tendencies. We all have them, acknowledged or not. And it takes even greater courage to address them. Like all growth opportunities, we can only address them when the catalyst for choosing is present. The level of discomfort (fear) often knee jerks us into regaining power in the old habitual ways. We revert to what we know best: control dramas. Hopefully, awareness of the ineffectual nature of this choice leads us to more meaningful, satisfying, honoring choices. Remember: we'll only choose a new way when we're under the pressure of a new situation, a new catalyst. Great courage and determination are required. This is truly tricky business with our wily ego's separating measures to win at all costs. We must hold tight to our desire for peace and joining, to find new ways to ensure it in all situations.

When we join with another, there is no victim, no separating manipulator present, no need to control another. You may have a preference in the situation but not an expectation upon which your happiness depends. We don't give away the power to choose happiness in this moment. We join with, honor ourselves and the other, and find our way together. This the magnificent power of choice, free will, used exquisitely. With this ability to choose, we're incredibly powerful beings who are greatly loved and supported by the Source Energy.

Summary of Key Ideas

- Manipulative ego-control dramas are formed when we're young as attempts to grab power when we feel powerless.

- The four control dramas, as depicted in James Redfield's *The Celestine Prophecy* are intimidator, interrogator, aloof, and poor me.

  o *Intimidator* attempts to gain power by appearing threatening, subtly or obviously.

  o *Interrogator* asks questions to find something to judge, disapprove, or correct.

  o *Aloof* withdraws, emotionally, psychologically or physically in order to be pursued.

  o *Poor Me* openly chooses another person or situation to blame for their unhappiness.

- Control dramas are always manipulative, dishonest communication.

- Recognizing control dramas, our own and others, requires honesty that will automatically shift the dynamics.

- Real help supports the person, not the misperception of responsibility and the problem. We support while the other person works to regain balance and decide what is next.

- Expectation has our happiness dependent upon it—we give our power away. Preference allows us to remain powerful choosers of our responses.

CHAPTER 5

To Know or Not to Know

Our peaceful countenance is a measure of how well we are connected with the energy. We stay connected because it is the best thing for us to do, regardless of the circumstances.

—James Redfield, *The Celestine Prophecy*

Control is one of our favorite ways of running from life as it is. Control is so deeply ingrained an illusion that we even think we can let go of control by simply wanting to. We do not let go of control; we let go of the belief that we have control. The rest is grace.

—David Richo

While it's difficult to accept, there's nothing before us but what we choose to see. Whatever we see is given the meaning by us, projected, and then perceived to be its reality. The meaning wasn't there first independent of our looking. It was given by us and then believed to be so, the "truth" of the situation. Again, there is no independent meaning or reality, no meaning or reality independent of perception. Truly. Quantum physics substantiates that in stating "the observer affects everything observed." That is absolutely true of every situation, as we're the observers who give everything the meaning it has for us. So, purposeful "not knowing" allows space to "know" in alignment with "true knowing," rather than be informed by ego, fear, and misperception.

It would be easy to confuse delaying the choice of perception as denial. If there is an "assumed" reality and we haven't agreed to that assumption, to withhold knowing may appear we're in denial, some would say like Pollyanna, not seeing what is truly before us. We're actually simply unknowing, open. We haven't denied anything, and we haven't assumed anything either.

Consider this example of how we quickly give meaning to what we see. Suppose we're out for a walk, and we see a non-serious traffic accident at the corner. There are others who are gathering. The police are there, and a newspaper reporter happens to be driving by and stops to see what has happened. The reporter, seeing a story and a need for accuracy, asks those who are watching to tell him what is going on. The nurse who is watching tells him that no one seems to be injured. The tow truck driver says that this will cost a lot in bodywork. The mother is so glad that the small children were both buckled and are safe. The lawyer refers to the liability involved. The officer seeks to find who is at fault. The person whose father was in an accident last week starts crying. Everyone's perspective is unique to his or her own history. We view everything in relation to our own life experiences and history. We supply the meaning to everything, informed by our experience!

As previously discussed, the process of perception is determined by the choice of interpretive lens. And remember: the choices—ego or aligned; separating or joining; fear or love; disturbance or happiness—are all the same choice in different description. We see something and then race into our historical, experiential mental files searching for meaning. We immediately project that meaning (forgetting instantly that we have done so) and believe that the projection is the truth of what we're seeing. It's the "truth" for us. And it's perceptually biased. This process is happening constantly. We're continually assigning meaning to what we see and believing it to be the "real" meaning. It may be a meaning that lots of folks agree upon, but the bias is still present—it's just consensual, collective meaning. We automatically project meaning for everything that we observe. When the meaning serves our happiness, there's no problem with this process. When it doesn't serve our happiness, when the meanings we project results in fear, guilt and pain, or any discomfort, we would be well served to not rely on our own knowing and seek another way.

Of course, the other way is to be willing to not know and to be willing to stay in the open place where judgment is held idle. Freedom is the willingness to not rush into judgmental, reactionary knowing, so that true, inner knowledge may emerge. Initially, as we learn to practice "not knowing," we'll probably feel very awkward and insecure. We're used to knowing. We're comfortable knowing. The ego knows. This false or limited knowing makes us feel secure, in control. We have been trained to know and to figure things out from our knowing.

What we're being asked to do here is counterintuitive, counterculture! We perceive our very safety is in knowing—everything! We have been trained to trust the thinking that serves as the basis for our knowing. Based on that idea, we're always going to be somewhat insecure if security is based on knowing. It's impossible to ever know it all. Though we sometimes pretend that we do. The good news is this doesn't mean that we can't know as needed. It means, instead, that we must hold back from premature ego believing we know, when we don't. True knowing is larger than this egoic process. It requires we develop a trust. We'll more fully pursue trust in truly knowing in chapter 12. Suffice it to say here that true knowing is a universal knowing that's given when we ask. It serves us to not preempt that asking by knowing from a limited perspective.

When we have projected meaning onto our experience and then believe we know what it means, it's obvious that we only know what we *think* it means. We have used ourselves as our own best resource and that, more often than not, is very short sighted. And to make matters worse, we're most apt to believe our ego-projected meaning in situations that are disturbing or stressful, the times when it would be most helpful to have a wider, more informed, view. We're most apt to rush in and "know" what is going on at those times when our minds aren't operating from a clear, balanced place because our emotional meters have begun to rise. The situation at hand has resonated with our uneasiness and we feel we need to hurry to "know" as a defensive tactic. Unfortunately, the more stressed we are, the higher our emotional meter registers, and the less available is our rational mind and good thinking.

When we're willing to pause the automatic stress response, perhaps, most easily, with a deep breath, we are less apt to rush to knowing prematurely. The added benefits that this pause allows our emotions to settle as well; we're less likely to be stuck in a fearful perspective. Most importantly, the willingness to "not know" creates an access to a much deeper knowing within us. This deeper knowing is connected to Inner Wisdom, Universal Knowledge, and can inform us in a way that our ego-thinking minds cannot. Some refer to this as inner guidance or intuitive guidance. We all have it, but most of us are not very practiced in accessing it. Fear and the need to "know" quickly, defensively, have kept this deeper knowing out of our awareness. To say it another way, our choices to be separate from one another has preoccupied our minds and kept us fearfully trapped in egoistic knowing. Since we cannot be in both aspects of our minds, ego or aligned, at the same time (cannot serve two masters), one is permitted always at the exclusion of the other.

Ego, or small self knowing, is restrictive. When I prematurely "know," I have also limited possible outcomes to what I expect. If I know what it means, I limit the possibilities for its manifestation into another form. Because perception is the creative element, if I think it's disastrous, it becomes disastrous. I get what I expect. The opportunities for another perspective have been precluded with my limited expectation. Freedom lies in not knowing without guidance, because only this knowing allows openness to all possibilities. That is scary for the ego, delicious to the true self.

Eventually, we learn that fear motivates a rush to know what things mean but that this kind of knowing is usually shortsighted. Accepting a situation, or simply observing it, allows "breathing room" to open to greater knowing. True knowing isn't without guidance. The tiny pause to take a breath interrupts the fearful, premature knowing process and allows us to access more informed knowing. And, yes, it takes practice to change our habitual ways and access that tiny pause. There is incredible freedom in not knowing and allowing ourselves to be guided. We learn to ride the wave rather than try to direct it to the shore!

Summary of Key Ideas

- There is no independent meaning for anything because there is no meaning independent of perception.
- We view everything in relation to our own life experiences, our histories. Collective or agreed upon meanings are just many doing the same process.
- We're continually assigning meaning to what we see and believe it to be the "real" meaning.
- When the meaning we project results in fear, guilt, and pain, we would be well served to not rely on our own knowing and seek another way.
- A deep breath interrupts the process of premature knowing.
- We cannot be in our judgmental and nonjudgmental minds at the same time; one is always present to the exclusion of the other.
- How we feel indicates which mind we're using in any moment. We're apt to believe our fearful projected meaning under stress.
- My premature knowing limits the outcome to my expectation.
- True, aligned knowing is informed by Inner Wisdom and supportive Source Energy. It requires our willingness to ask and be informed.
- Freedom is the willingness to not rush into judgmental, reactionary knowing so that true, inner knowledge may emerge.
- True knowing isn't without Guidance, and it allows all possibilities.

CHAPTER 6
Two Minds, Two Perspectives

Between stimulus and response, there is a space. In that space is our power to choose our response. In our response lies our growth and our freedom.

—Viktor Frankl

The conscious use of intent is the key to the next leap in human evolution. To grasp the meaning of this, we need to realize that our true human potential has not yet been developed due to the devastating consequences of our individual and collective false perceptions. We must act knowing that our intentions create the world, rather than feeling like we are being acted upon by outside forces beyond our control.

—Judith Bluestone Polich, *Return of the Children of Light*

While we haven't addressed the two aspects of our minds directly, you can probably surmise from the previous discussion what they are. The separating choice of mind, the ego, or small self, directs us to see ourselves from a me-first perspective. The ego mind, self, is always looking out for what seems best for me in the moment. The ego self is the "getting" focus in the mind. Its wealth is in the physical world, and its happiness is related to the acquisition of people, things, and perceived power. This ego self believes that its gain is your loss, there is only so much, and that it is more deserving than you are. Consequently, it believes you think this way too, so we'll have to be fearful of each other to get what we want and keep it. This, of course, is the source of our desire to use manipulating behaviors. The fuels of the ego mind are the ideas of sin (misperception in its truest definition), control, guilt, and fear. These are the weapons it will use to create victim perspectives. The self-serving ego is the belief in separation, and these three aspects—sin, guilt and fear—are what maintain the idea of separation. Through attack and defense, separation is perceived and maintained.

Conversely, the joining choice, the aligned mind, or the True Self, is that which sees us collectively. The True Self recognizes we're all one and what I see in you is an aspect of me and projected by me! It knows we're much more than these physical bodies, and the truth of us is something more expansive. The aligned mind's focus is on giving. It's aware that everything given is received as well, for they are two parts of the same process. It believes that abundance is in the mind and not simply a concept of physical acquisition or power over. It believes in power with. It knows that happiness and well-being are the greatest richness and understands it can only be achieved by joining with, never separating from.

These two perspectives represent the duality of human experience. We're always vacillating between these two mind perspectives—constantly. We have lived most of our lives in the clutches of the separating ego mind unaware that there was another alternative. Not only is there another alternative, but it's actually the truth of who we are, and the separating ego mind is an illusion whose unreality we have failed to notice. We have been so occupied with separation, the business of attack and defense, the smokescreen of the ego, that the truth of us has been hidden from our sight by our own choice not to see! We live in amazing times, and we're waking up. We're awakening from the illusory dream of being separate bodies to recognizing we're indeed one in spirit and one with our creative Source.

It might actually be said another way also. If we have given the separating ego perspective free rein in our lives, we have served the ego through our fear of loss of control. Because we cannot ever gain control over the physical world, we surrender our happiness to the need to control. If we truly wish to be happy, we'll be in service to our aligned, joining minds. We need the ego, but we don't need to be controlled by its separating choices. We use the ego's awareness of the physical aspect of living in service to joining, to the well-being of all.

If you have been drawn to these ideas, it isn't by accident. You're aware of these pregnant times in which we live and are in the process of uncovering your True Self. We're actually all doing this—some of us are aware that we're awakening, and some of us are not yet aware. For those who are aware, the process is more deliberate because we've finally recognized the power of choice, the innate power of free will. That power to choose our perspective—the fearful, separating, ego mind, or the peaceful, joining, loving, aligned mind. It's the only true power. Choice alone fuels our balance, our peace, and our happiness—or our lack of it.

We might liken this time to having been on a battlefield doing everything in our power to survive. We were so engaged in the battle that we had little time to consider another way of living. We had to keep attacking and defending in order to stay alive. Becoming aware of the power to choose (our free will) allows us to encounter the battlefield from a different perspective. We add the element of observer or witness to our skills. So we no longer just keep on slugging away, fearing in every moment for our demise. Instead, we watch ourselves in action and evaluate the choices we're making. We observe their effectiveness and have the space to consider options. This little bit of step-back space allows a connection to that deeper knowing, to the Universal Mind, and we begin to sense that we're no longer on our own and separate. The more we're willing to step back into the role of the observer, to not know, the more open we become to the input of the One Mind, the input of true knowing.

When we refuse victim perspectives, we step off the battlefield. We reject separation and the disempowering idea of you against me. When we're unwilling to perceive ourselves unfairly treated, we have no need for defense or counterattack. Instead, we take no frustrating ego-separating detours but join with the situation and the people involved to consider what is next. We waste no time and energy in assigning blame or lamenting the conditions. We simply move to what is next and in the best interest of us all. There is a sense of satisfaction, joy, and peace, even safety, in this joined alliance. We're at one with each other, and all is truly well. When we're joined together, we're at peace—independent of the physical circumstances. Physical circumstances will never be consistently aligned for our eternal happiness. We must stop waiting for it to be so and be happy anyhow. It's within our power!

Summary of Key Ideas

- In the duality of human experience, we're always vacillating between two mind perspectives: the ego mind (self) and the aligned mind (True Self). Another way to express this is the getting mind and the giving mind.
- The ego-self is the "getting," separating focus of the mind. The ego mind believes that its gain is your loss. There is only so much, and that I'm more deserving than you are.
- The ego is the belief in separation. Sin, guilt, and fear maintain the idea of separation. The ego mind is an illusion whose unreality we have failed to notice.
- The aligned mind, True Self, recognizes we're all one and that what I see in you is a projected aspect of me. The aligned mind is love, and its focus is giving,—expanding love.
- We're awakening from the illusory dream of being separate bodies to the reality of our spiritual unity and alignment. We're created by love and supported by love.
- That power to choose our perspective (the fearful, separating, ego mind or the peaceful, joining, aligned mind) is the only true power.
- Free will and choice fuel our happiness and peace, or our lack of it.
- When we're joined together, we feel balanced and peaceful, independent of the physical circumstances.

CHAPTER 7

Everything is Opportunity— No Problem

A difficult and challenging time must be taken as an opportunity to express in the outer world our highest inner principle.

—*The I Ching or Book of Changes,* Brian Brown Walker

Trials are but lessons that you failed to learn presented once again...

—*A Course in Miracles*

Each encounter is unprecedented; each encounter is unrepeatable. Treasure each encounter.

—Eido Tai Shimano Rossi

When we have a "problem," it can't be created without a choice to perceive something as problematic. We might say we have an intention or direction of focus. In every situation, it's that choice of perception, or intention of mind, that leads to our experience. We intend, usually unconsciously, to be joined and peaceful, or we don't. Problematic perception leads to uncomfortable separating experiences. Therefore, the person with the problem is the person with the problem. Problems to not exist without a perception of them.

There is only this one choice that is persistently before us. We express it with a myriad of descriptive contrasting terms: joining or separation, love or fear, peace or conflict, comfort or distress, happiness or upset, truth or illusions, and so on. We're forever making that same choice of intention, whatever the verbiage we use for description. We create our own outcome from the choice of perception or intention with every life experience.

Absolutely every situation that comes is this one opportunity of choice, or intent, presenting itself in yet another life drama. Only the characters and the apparent physical circumstances change. We could say that learning to make the perceptual choice that consistently leads to happiness is our life's work. Our challenge, of course, is that we so often neglect to make the peaceful choice of perception. We learn it's the wrong choice by recognizing the discomfort that always follows. Recognizing the option of this choice is greatly complicated by the fact that we're regularly hooked by the drama of individual circumstances. In the perceived drama, we forget the opportunity for choosing that resides within each situation. To say it another way, when we focus on the perceived "problem" and its resolution, we forget we could choose to perceive differently and the "problem" would disappear, simply to be seen as opportunity to choose again, Remember: the "problem" is a construct of perception projected onto the situation and seen as real. It's illusory, truly a figment of our imaginations.

We hold a problem in place by our attention to it. This is so difficult to accept, isn't it? We really want to argue that some situations are really real! The more distressing they seem, the more we believe in their reality! Again, remember: they can only be distressing by our evaluation (judgment), and our evaluation comes from our "knowing" projected onto the situation and seen as real. "Projection makes perception" (*A Course in Miracles*). Our willingness to refrain from judgmental knowing precludes problem formation. We can't have a problem without "knowing," or believing, we have one.

We're not talking about denial here, although it could be misconstrued as such. Denial would be to see something and then pretend that you didn't see it. Often, we do this below the level of our conscious awareness. What we're talking about as "not knowing" is the willingness to observe and, at the same time, withhold the fearful, knee-jerk, ego mind search to determine and apply meaning (projection) prematurely. Remember from our earlier discussion that, at the stimulation of every new situation, the ego's default programming fearfully races into the search for meaning in the mental files of personal history to abate its fear. Next, it selects what the situation resonates in its experience base and says, *This must be what it means now*, and applies that meaning to the current situation. It then reacts to the meaning that has been projected. If it selects in error, which it always does, because it takes everything personally, then the whole situation becomes skewed. This is why, from the ego perspective, we fearfully perceive that persons or situations are attacking us or are in resistance to us.

It's important to reiterate that nothing that appears to be happening to us is personal. It only becomes personal in our engagement with it through the story we tell about it. In the previous fictional example of the person interrupting me in my office, it happened independent of me even though it was experienced by me. It only becomes about me if I think it's about me! When I simply observe it, I see something going on and deal with it but never have to become upset with it or feel attacked about it. It just is (was; it's over if I'm observing it), and I do what is next.

The larger the drama, the more difficult it is to not take personally. Let's take it up a notch as far as perceived seriousness of the situation. There is an interesting book by Carolyn Miller entitled *Creating Miracles*. In the first chapters of this book, the author tells story after story of events that had the space to unfold differently than expected. The difference occurred because one of the participants, the one seen as the "potential" victim, didn't behave as a victim "should." They were, instead, willing to join with the potential "victimizers," and the entire drama took a different direction.

I remember the story of a young woman who was returning to her apartment late at night. As she parked her car and got out, two men approached her and told her they were going to rape her. She, amazingly, held fear at bay and decided to be as peaceful as possible and as joining as possible. She tells them something to this effect, "What a bummer. I just bought this outfit, and it cost me a lot of money! Let's go over to my apartment and at least let me save the clothes." She hopes this joining will create some forthcoming shift in the tide of events. On the way across the parking lot, she chats with them. When they get to the door of her apartment, they stop and say to her, "You know, you should really be careful late at night and not come home unescorted." And they leave! Her unwillingness to know what it all meant allowed the space for it to unfold differently.

I remember a similar event told one night in a group study I was facilitating where we had talked about this book and the phenomena. One of the participants was a lovely, young, newly married woman who lived in a downtown apartment right behind the district court, a less busy area at night. It was a summer evening. She had parked her car in the nearby lot and was walking the short distance to her apartment doorway. As she got closer to her doorway, she saw two very big men loitering there. At first, she was frightened but then remembered the discussion in our group about "not knowing." She asked Spirit to guide her thinking and allow her to remain peaceful. She said it was an amazing experience. When she got to the doorway, it seemed these words to one of the men just came effortlessly out of her mouth: "That is the best hair I have seen in ten years!" They all laughed, the men stepped aside to make way for her entrance, and there was no problem. There was no problem because, with Spirit's help, she refused to see a problem. She chose to join instead. This is always an option for all of us. Problems don't have lives of their own. They don't just happen to us. They are not independent of our thinking. Remember that they are constructs of our minds projected onto situations. Absolutely nothing has the power to separate us from our happiness without our own participation. Happiness is indeed a choice, one that we must be willing to make again and again as we meet every situation of our lives. When *A Course in Miracles* states, "You're doing this unto yourself," that's what it's saying. The ego choice for a problematic perception is our own doing. We have another choice.

> *There are opportunities even in the most difficult moments.*
>
> —Wangari Maatha

"No problem" literally means no perception of problem! It vocalizes the choice to refuse a problem orientation. We've all done this many times. With practice, we'll see everything as no problem and, instead, see the opportunity to be happy that resides within every situation. With enthusiasm, we can look forward to the day when we'll eagerly embrace everything as simply the opportunity to practice happiness. No-problem perspectives speed us on our way.

Our ego ways of perceiving are often quite subtle and easily slip below the notice of our consciousness awareness. That is certainly true with the habitual ways we all have of setting up problem perspectives. One of the ways we do this is by having expectations. Expectations are another disguise for our knowing. Expectation is knowing how things "should be," how they "should" evolve. More truthfully, they are expressions of how we want things to be—we often manipulatively call this the "right way." As was said before, being right is always at the expense of being happy. Expectations say that I will be happy *if* things turn out this way, the right way, as judged by me. The basic error in assumption here is that I know what is the perfect, right way for things to turn out. It is, of course, only the ego separated mind who could know this and to be sure, it would be in concert with what it would personally see as beneficial—often at someone else's expense.

In addition, expectations prohibit us from being present in this moment. Instead, we're focused ahead on what we want in the future and forfeit the joy of the right now. Seneca said it well when he said, "Expectation is the greatest impediment to living. In anticipation of tomorrow, it loses today." We lose the present moment in anticipating a future moment.

The loving mind is open to everyone receiving, and avoids limiting the outcome by holding any personal expectations. It might have a preference, but preferences differ greatly from expectations in that happiness doesn't hinge upon them. Preferences recognize that, of what is seen, this looks like the best option, but I'm willing to stay open for a larger selection! Recognizing when we're holding expectations and being willing to deescalate them to the level of preference is a critical step in choosing happiness.

Summary of Key Ideas

- Choice of perception, or intention of mind, leads to our experience.

- There are only two choices said many ways: joining or separating; love or fear; peace or conflict; comfort or distress; happiness or upset; truth or illusions; and so on.

- We can learn to make the perceptual choice that leads to happiness. It's our life's work.

- Focusing on the perceived "problem" and its resolution allows us to forget we have the choice to perceive differently and the "problem" would disappear.

- A problem is a perception projected onto the situation and seen as "real." Problems are held in place by our perceptual attention.

- Denial is to see something and then pretend that you didn't see it.

- "Not knowing" is the willingness to observe and, at the same time, withhold the ego mind search to determine and apply meaning (projection) prematurely.

- Nothing that appears to be happening to us is personal. It only becomes personal as we engage with it, and therefore choose to separate from happiness!

- With expectation, our happiness is dependent on a preconceived outcome.

- Being "right" is always at the expense of being happy.

- Every new situation is simply the opportunity to choose—our free will.

- We choose what everything means!

CHAPTER 8

Getting "Hooked Up"

And I said to the man who stood at the gate of the year, "Give me a light that I may tread safely into the unknown." And he replied, "Go out into the darkness and put your hand into the hand of God. That shall be to you better than a light and safer than a known way."

—Minnie Louise Haskins

We have to attain a fuller consciousness, an inner connection with God, because only then can our evolution toward something better be guided by a higher part of ourselves.

—James Redfield, *The Celestine Prophecy*

There is a community for the spirit. Join it and feel the delight.

—Rumi

We have talked a great deal about the importance of not knowing, which creates the space to allow true knowing to emerge. Inner Wisdom has been frequently mentioned as the source of true knowing, and that is indeed the case. What is that inner wisdom, and where does it come from? How is it that some people seem to be better connected to it than others? And why when we try hard or really want to access it does it seem the most elusive.

Well, let me first say that you're hearing one person's perspective. What I'm about to say is the ultimate truth for me, but may not be relevant to your view. That is perfectly fine with me. We all see these intangible realities from our tangible perspectives, and we're doing the best we can to capture their essence. After all, these are just words on paper, collected to talk about a level of being (existence) that's beyond words. I'll do my best to convey my perceived meaning and you do your best to get the gist of it. If we can do that, we'll have accomplished a great deal together.

Inner wisdom is really Inner Wisdom. It's that Divine identity of us that's the real truth of who/what we are. I believe we're divine sparks, energetic creations, of a Divine Creator and, in being so, are forever part of that Divinity, forever divine. A good analogy is the drops of the ocean. While individual momentarily, they're always still ocean, or the rays of sunshine, while shining in a particular way in a particular place, always remain part of the sun energy as a whole. This spiritual essence is our truest nature, and unlike the body, it's unassailable and unchangeable. We are and always will be a divine part of a Divine Whole.

We may see a lot of folks who don't look very divine to us, and at times, we don't feel so divine ourselves. Nevertheless, it still holds. No matter what behaviors we, or others, may be exhibiting, the spiritual truth of us is unaffected. We experience that truth when we're happy and peaceful, when we feel connected to well-being and are feeling satisfied—if only for a moment. That is what peace or happiness is—simply, the lack of striving for it. For a brief period, we have everything we want, and we know it. In those moments, we're placing no judgments upon others or ourselves. We simply are. We're seeking nothing; we're enjoying everything. We're naturally extending our vibrations of peacefulness and happiness, and all is well. You might say that, in those moments, we're the most aligned with our True Self and simply allowing it to flow through the vessel of our physical being and experience.

Conversely, when we're in some place of striving, controlling, or getting, we're temporarily unaware of that truer peaceful divinity. For some of us, that's true for an entire lifetime. In those moments our divinity seems but a fleeting idea, if considered at all. But that doesn't mean the divine truth of us isn't so. It just means that for the time being, our focus isn't on it—we've forgotten it. It never goes away, but we can unwittingly block it from conscious awareness. We have usually been distracted by some perception of conflict or problem.

We're so much more than a physical body. In fact, this truth of us, as divine beings, has very little to do with physical bodies. And yet, on this plane of dualistic perception, it's easy to believe that we're physical bodies. As Wayne Dyer said so well, "We're spiritual beings having physical experiences," not the other way around. In this dualistic physical reality, the body gives mobility, reception, communication, and creative abilities for nonphysical self-expression in terms that we and other physical beings can perceive. It's a temporary vehicle. The true nature of us is eternal, unchangeable, and completely unassailable!

When I'm attached to a drama in the physical world, my own or that of someone else, I'm temporarily, unconsciously denying our true spiritual reality. My perception cannot serve two masters. I will be aware of myself as a separate, physical being *or* as a divine, spiritual being using the physical. In any one moment, I will give my attention to one perception of myself or the other. I will know what I'm choosing in any instant by noticing how I feel. If I'm happy, peaceful, allowing, content, and so on, I'm acknowledging my divine truth, and it shines forth of its own accord. However, if I'm feeling upset or discomforted in any way, it's testimony to my having chosen an ego perception of physical separation and fear as my reality. When I make that choice, my truth is hidden from sight, much like the clouds hide the sun on a cloudy day. The sun is still there; we just don't see it. Intellectually, it's obvious that only one choice really makes any sense, the choice for happiness, peace, alignment.

We are, however, very practiced in making the ego-driven, fearful choice leading to discomfort and upset. We so often feel separated and victimized. Intrinsic to our separating view is the belief in our identity as bodies only. For how could we victimize or separate from a spiritual reality? It isn't possible. That is why the truth of us cannot be attacked—only the illusion of us as a body is subject to attack and change. Getting clear on who we really are helps us to sit back and not react. Instead, we observe and peacefully respond to all the events of our physical experiences. We can have our preferred outcomes, but we sit peacefully in the knowledge of our eternal divinity and simply choose to do what is next in each physical situation. Our spiritual invulnerability is a great blessing once we recognize and accept it. Practice, practice, practice!

So, inner wisdom is the acknowledgement of Inner Wisdom and the truth of us all as divine beings. It's a connection to Universal Mind and the awareness that we're all energetically connected like the droplets in the ocean or the rays of the sun. It's a mind energy that is open to the energy of all minds because, in truth, it's just One Mind available to all. We might say it's Source Energy forever being expanded by each of us in expression. It's unlimited and eternal, which makes us the same! Amazing concept isn't it? Through the power of choosing openness to unlimited perception, our ultimate truth as spiritual beings, we become unlimited and fearless! When we truly allow that connection by choice, Source Energy does what it does, and limitlessly flows through us. We truly need do nothing but choose to allow it. Most of us do know that experience, however fleeting and infrequent it may be.

How is it that some people seem to be better connected to Source Energy than others? By now, that answer must be obvious. We're as connected to Inner Wisdom as we care to be. Free will.

We allow in what we choose to allow in. There are no overrides; Inner Wisdom never forces itself into our awareness. We allow, and we receive; we don't open to it, and we don't experience it. The power of this choice is the ultimate power.

What about grace? It seems to me that occasionally we're vibrationally, though not consciously, open to another way. The gift of a greater knowing at those times is what grace is to me. At some level, I have been open to a more aligned perspective. I certainly believe in grace, am open to grace, but don't presume to know the dynamics allowing it.

Why is it that when we really want to connect with Source and try hard, it seems most evasive? Trying isn't allowing. Trying is expending effort to get something. In actuality, it's resistance to the something. Do you see that? It's an evasive concept. Trying presumes that what we want is difficult to obtain and must be overcome to gain it. Allowing, on the other hand, simply lets in what is already flowing toward us. The nature of Inner Wisdom is to give all to all. Our part is to simply remove the interference. Trying, effort, doubt, problems, conflict, despair, and all the forms of negative, separating perception are the constituents of interference. Allowing focuses on none of that and simply opens to receive. Inner Wisdom is constantly being offered. Are we open and willing to let it in?

Summary of Key Ideas

- We're divine sparks (energetic creations) of a Divine Creator and, in being so, are forever part of that divinity, forever divine.
- Our spiritual essence is our true nature, and unlike the body, it's unassailable and unchangeable.
- We experience our true nature when we're happy and peaceful. When we're striving, controlling or getting, and so on, we're unaware of our nature as peaceful, divine beings.
- The body is a temporary vehicle for communication and expression, our true natures as spiritual beings is eternal.
- My perception cannot serve two masters. I will be aware of myself as a separate, physical being, a body; or a divine, spiritual being, greater than a body and an aspect of Wholeness.
- My feelings let me know which perception I'm choosing. The power of choice is the ultimate power; the inherent gift of free will.
- The truth of us cannot be attacked. Only the illusion of us as a body is subject to attack and change.
- Inner Wisdom is a mind energy that's available to all. We're as connected to Inner Wisdom as we care to be.
- Trying presumes that what we want is difficult to obtain. Allowing, on the other hand, simply lets in what is already available to us.

CHAPTER 9

Sacrifice or Gift

*Learn now that sacrifice of any kind is nothing but a
limitation imposed on giving ... For if there is sacrifice,
someone must pay and someone must get ... sacrifice is
attack, not love.*

—*A Course in Miracles*

As challenging as it may be to accept, we always behave as we do
because we chose to do so. In any particular moment, we always
do what we do because we want to. We don't do it because we
need to, have to, should, are made to, have no other choice, and
so on. We always simply want to do that particular thing in this
moment of time. Perceiving it any other way is our feeble attempt
to project responsibility for our choice of behavior and blame it
on something, someone, or some circumstance external to us and
"beyond our control."

Remember: everything external to us *is* beyond our control.
We must come to accept the fact that we absolutely cannot control
external circumstances. We can only control our responses to
them. So, to project blame onto anything is an attempt to deny the
above facts—and believe we're victimized. When we don't want
to take responsibility for the choice we're making; we create a
victim posture—a projected story to eliminate our own perceptual
responsibility. We make a smokescreen, usually some form of
anger or wounded posture, so we won't have to be accountable

for the choice. It's an attempt to hide our responsibility for the choice from others but, even more importantly, from ourselves.

We're not wrong when we do this. We're temporarily lost from our truth, our True Self. Fear of responsibility has prompted the current choice. We feel separate and afraid. We have forgotten our truth—again. We falsely believed, once more, that we could be separate and apart from our Source—which is the mistaken ego perspective. That separation is impossible! We're an aspect of Source Energy; we're the divine of The Divine. Fear is the only thing that enlivens and recreates the belief in separation, which always diverts us from seeing our true nature. In the habitual patterns of ego behavior, we're given constant opportunities for choosing differently. This life is, most importantly, the experience of learning that new choice. It's the choice for joining and wholeness which recognizes the truth of ourselves.

In the big picture, what a magnificent, tremendous gift choice is. The gift of free will, the ability to see differently through choice, provides us with the option to change the appearance of circumstances, at will, by a shift in perception. Remember: external circumstances are only what we make of them by our choice of perception. When we see from our wholeness, every discomforting experience is the opportunity to practice peace again. When we see from our separateness, those same circumstances are something to be controlled and resisted, we're victimized by them. Seen from the larger perspective, each new circumstance is, again, the opportunity to remember that we're truly divine energetic beings endowed with choice. We use a body for experiencing and expression but we're not that body, we're just using it.

When we can grasp our spiritual nature and the endowment of choice, we begin to free ourselves from the tyranny of believing we're a body. That belief in ourselves as a body is tantamount to the belief in separation. That belief in ourselves as a body firmly establishes the ego and all the fears associated with it. A body believed as solely constituting *me* is the ultimate physical demonstration of separateness and having no choice! In truth, we're not physical or separate. All fears are victim, body fears; fears about that which might/will happen to the body, the largest of which is its demise—death.

As we move, more and more, into the realization that we're not the body, but a divine eternal energy lovingly inhabiting the body, our fearful natures begin to soften. This, of course, is a lifelong process for each of us. It's the "work" of this dualistic, earthly experience. We're here, in this earthly incarnation, to move from fear to love; separation to wholeness; discomfort to happiness. We're meant to be happy and have a magnificent process to wake up and create our own happiness. The process of our awakening is what it is. Fear is big stuff for everybody—as our separating behaviors testify. Only our willingness to recognize fear's compromising dynamics (anger, frustration, manipulation, etc.) and our willingness to choose differently will loosen its grip. We're powerful creators of our reality with this ability to choose again.

It takes great courage to confront our fearful habits. Be grateful for every tiny step taken on the path to freedom from the fearful ego. The choice for emancipation from fear, the belief in separation, and the ego, is presented in every discomforting situation. We face the choice for peace in each opportunity that discomfort signals. We must celebrate each moment we take ourselves out of fear's grip by choosing peace. In each of these moments, our happiness, our eternal reality, is being realized and the incredible power of choice is revealed again. We're literally growing into our truth.

Remember: we always choose our behaviors and we'll either take responsibility for the choice or project responsibility for the choice, depending upon the current level of fear. Where does the idea of sacrifice fit? We probably have been taught that sacrifice is a good thing, a kindness we do because it benefits another.

Perhaps the idea of sacrifice has been misunderstood—for a very long time.

Sacrifice is the ultimate smokescreen. Inherently, it denies there was an opportunity to choose. We "had to do this" for some "good" reason. The perception is that we did it for you at the cost of us. It was better for you if I did this. Really? We must not fool ourselves into believing this projection of responsibility is anything but just that—a blaming of my choice of behavior on some person or circumstance external to me and beyond my control. Hogwash! Not possible! We did what we wanted to do, couldn't take responsibility for it, and tried to create a smokescreen so we would look "good." Pure ego. All fearful victim behavior. We always do what we want to do in the moment. Only that. We're our own chooser. We do what we want by virtue of the fact that we're the chooser. If we didn't want to do that, we would have done something else. Reasons for choosing don't matter. We can deny responsibility for the choice but we still were the only one making it. By virtue of the fact that we made the choice, it was what we wanted in that moment in time—or we would have chosen differently!

When we can accept that we choose what we want to choose, free will, we'll realize our every choice has the potential for being our gift to life in that moment, not our sacrifice to life— our gift to it! The energy in that shift of awareness is incredible and enormous! We move from burdensome, separating, guilty, fearful, getting energy to full, expanding, joining, giving energy. And with that shift, peace and happiness return.

Sacrifice is heavy and has so much guilt and fear associated with it. It's a victim posture slid in under the guise of "goodness." "I'm so good to give up what I want to give you what you want/ need instead." Always hidden in that idea is "Now I'm one up. You owe me." This fact is rarely admitted into consciousness but is always present. By my needing to do this for you (you poor thing, read: victim) I have victimized you through the selection of you as the object of my projection. You're why I had to do this. You have been manipulated by me and now experience guilt and obligation. You subtly resent this action and this "giver" but don't know why. You may not even recognize the resentment because wouldn't it be ungrateful in response to what I just did "for" you? It's all ego drama and manipulation by guilt. It's a power play and not pretty. It contains *no* goodness. Be clear. There is no loving giving in sacrifice!

Conversely, when we accept responsibility for our choice, when we do what we do because we want to do it, our choice is a gift with no strings attached. It's a demonstration of loving giving which wants nothing in return. It's offered in a spirit of joining, of sharing, of connecting, of love. There is no manipulation in true giving. Loving giving has no expectation attached to it. It's given freely because we chose to do so. Consider what a blessing that is to both the giver and the receiver. Both are expanded in love.

To stretch this concept to the max, what if we viewed the crucifixion as a gift rather than a sacrifice. Pretty radical! Blasphemous? Hang on, perhaps not. If Jesus, like us, was the divine of the Divine, in his wholeness, would He have wanted to create more guilt and fear through sacrifice? Would a loving God Energy have been able to be unloving for a moment and be sacrificial? It just doesn't compute. That never made sense to me since I was a young girl. How could Ultimate Love not be loving?

What has come to be my awareness now is that the crucifixion was an amazing gift, the ultimate demonstration of love in the face of what we perceive as extreme bodily harm. Was the bodily harm experienced as harmful if Jesus fully knew he was not a body? Perhaps the recorders (perceivers) of this event told it from their perspective of sacrifice instead of Love's perspective of giving.

As the story is recorded, Jesus never spoke in his own defense. He seemed to be completely willing to offer the body in this outrageous demonstration of prevailing love. He seemed to know Who He Was as an eternal, impenetrable, and invulnerable spiritual being. He wasn't the body, which, in its physicalness, is none of the above. Perhaps the crucifixion was a tremendous and much-needed teaching for humanity—then and now.

Perhaps, the reality of love was taught in the crucifixion experience? He taught what He, and we, truly are—love. There was no confusion with the body, though those witnessing were very confused and reported from their confusion. Their fear was projected onto the situation. It's a human erroneous habit. A new teaching was needed. The crucifixion was a much-needed teaching tool that we might go and do likewise in far less extreme circumstances. It demonstrated the nature of gift—not sacrifice. It was given freely and without expectation of return. It was given as a light upon the path to happiness and peace that we so desire. Perhaps we have been mistaken in our interpretation of that event.

Being mindful of our own propensity to sacrifice, and remembering it isn't a gift, will keep us on the path to happiness. Gift is joining—sacrifice is separation. Only one is accomplished through the spiritual connection with another. The other perpetuates the belief that we are, instead, separate from each other and have to be afraid of each other. Joining recognizes the equal worth of all of us. Separation highlights "me" as the focusing center of everything. Love, peace and happiness reside in giving, in joining—the expansion of love. Love's only characteristic is expansion, becoming more. What a gift!

Summary of Ideas

- We always do what we do because we want to.
- We cannot control external circumstances. We can only control our response to the circumstances.
- Fear is the only thing that maintains the belief in separation (the ego, the self).
- All fears are victim, body fears. They are fears about that which might/will happen to the body—its demise, its death.
- We're given constant earthly opportunities for choosing differently.
- The gift of free will, the ability to see differently through choice, provides us with the option to change our circumstances, at will, by changing our perception of them.
- Each new circumstance is, again, the opportunity to remember (recognize) that we're truly divine energetic beings.
- We're here in this earthly incarnation to move from fear to love; separation to wholeness; discomfort to happiness.
- Sacrifice is the ultimate smokescreen. It denies there was an opportunity to choose. We do what we want by virtue of the fact that we're the chooser.
- There is no loving giving in sacrifice! There is no manipulation in true giving.

CHAPTER 10

Feelings are Choice Alerts

*When you practice good-feeling thoughts and are,
therefore, more in control of your vibrational atmosphere,
then you are able to respond to the things that are
happening in the world from your practiced place of
alignment rather than from a reactionary place.*

—Abraham-Hicks

*It sounds so easy, maybe it is:
Stop doing the things that bring pain.
Start doing the things that bring happiness.*

—Daniel Levin, *Zen Life*

When talking with a friend the other day, he was commenting on news events. My response indicated my awareness of such events but not following them closely. He was astounded to hear that daily news was not routinely followed by me. My perspective is that what needs to be known will come into awareness. He thought that a completely irresponsible position. My comment to him was that, to me, it seemed completely responsible in the largest way possible.

The dissonant perspectives were contrasting and obviously uncomfortable. We had differing perspectives about following the news. Another friend has brought this same issue to my awareness, stating perhaps that I was just sticking my head in the sand. If the primary focus and goal in life is to be happy and peaceful, adding a positive energy to life, for me, news generally feels less than positive. Therefore, it seems wise not to imbibe. Giving great focus to what isn't going well in the material world, usually doesn't enhance one's happiness or peace. Giving undue attention to the negativity, also energetically, vibrationally expands what is currently being delivered as problematic in the world. Perhaps, not a helpful practice. What we think about expands, it has a vibration.

If we wish to be truly helpful, surely we don't become problem conscious and add vibrational energy to what we don't want. If the "problem," current newsworthy item is in the realm of offering tangible help, we'll consider what to do. If it isn't, we can focus on the possible changes that may be helpful. We can ask, "Help me to see this differently." There is a recent memory of listening to a report on a current war, and then, of course, feeling discomfort. In applying this strategy, there was awareness of what could be done with my own tendency to push against, be right, and "war" with another's opinion or perspective. In other words, to see my option to notice, and mend my own warring, separating behaviors. We all wish to be in alignment with each other in our deepest desires. How do we remember that in every interaction? We pay attention to how we feel. My discomforting reaction to the news reminded me of the opportunity to choose again. Everything is opportunity!

Author Michael Ryce speaks of the body's importance as "an evidential learning device." Through the body, we become aware of this internal "early warning system," our feelings. Unpleasant, discomforting feelings indicate a change of perception is needed. Discomfort is some form of fear. That fear is always related to the external world being out of our control. This is the ego's basis for all fear. It is, again, serving notice through *dis-ease*. We can't control externals. We'll never be able to control externals. We can control our response to externals. Discomfort serves notice that, once again, realignment is needed. Most of us need help in that process of realignment. Asking for help in changing perspective initiates true help. "Help me to see this differently," sends us on the way to peace again.

When I pay attention to any discomfort, I remember the sequence of projected thought and know my role in the projection, as the director of it. It's time to choose again, if I truly wish to return to equanimity and peace. Peace is *always* possible with a change of mind. We're the only choosers in our life. What amazing power.

Back to my friend and the news. My stated (yes, judgmental) perspective was that the news seems biased, negative and sensational. It often seems that the newsworthy is about what we don't want rather than what we do want. It generally doesn't feel good to me. For me, through some other process, what needs to be known generally arrives. Further pursuit of information may follow. When my friend and I continued the discussion, it moved to the idea that we always have the choice to promote well-being and happiness by offering a vibration that supports life rather than depletes it.

This, of course, applies to non-broadcast news as well. All information coming to us from the outside world has the perspective of the informant. Noticing how we feel about it leads us to wise decision making about what follows. Does another's or a group's choice of content and opinion serve our well-being, our peace, our happiness? If it doesn't, discomfort will be our clue to recognize, once again, the opportunity to see differently and to reclaim our peace—through choice.

Sometimes that discomfort is so tiny as to be almost imperceptible. We might call that the "niggle of disturbance." A niggle is just a twinge, a tweak of discomfort or annoyance that slips by, often unnoticed. It's a subtle attention getter, a wee signal to "Listen up!" The niggle is the first clue that we're perceiving from something other than love. Of course, the only other choice is the always-fearful, ego perspective. The niggle is the signal we're sitting in an ego perspective. It's the choice alert to exercise our free will and chose again. Time to get realigned with peace. What does this look like practically? An example:

Suppose, among my office workers, I'm the one who has agreed to purchase the coffee. One morning, I arrive for work, and my coworker greets me with, "I can't believe you let the coffee run out!" This is the discomforting catalyst. It's true., I have failed to get coffee in time. The niggle of disturbance isn't just about coffee—it's also about how this information is being shared. In fact, my niggle of disturbance is probably mostly about the "how."

Let's remember: at every point, we choose the lens of perception. Separating ego or joining alignment. If I got up late, dripped toothpaste on my blouse, and found water on my hairbrush, I probably already am looking through the lens of fear. Thus, the fearful meaning I will project onto this new situation is that it's just one more disaster in an already horrible day. I will feel attacked by this person, because I believe everything is attacking me today, and I will react in some defensive manner. To the catalyst, "I can't believe you let the coffee run out!" my fearful counterattack, self-defense, could be any number of responses:

- "Well, you can believe it!"
- "Well, somedays, I can't do everything."
- "You can't talk to me like that."
- "I'm not doing this job anymore. Maybe you can worry about it for a while."

These are all separating responses and maintain or expand the problem by giving more negative energy to it. Separating responses delay resolution.

Conversely, if I got up in time, had a nice breakfast and listened to my favorite radio station on the drive in, I may respond to the same catalyst, "I can't believe you let the coffee run out!" in a joining way. I don't let it be personal and move on:

- "Oh man, I guess we're going to have to believe it. What a bummer."
- "Oh, you're kidding. Bet that was a blow to come in and find no coffee!"
- "I bet you would like to fire me from this chore."
- "What shall we do now?" Or,
- "I'll go for coffee?"

These are all joining responses that accept the situation and go directly to what's next, the solution. We figure that out together. Discomfort is using the body as the evidential learning device. It reliably serves notice, the niggle of discomforting feelings, when it's time to choose again. This process of choosing to align with, rather than resist the situation, is what our growth experience is always offering. It's the path leading us to the truth of ourselves as beings of love.

On the path of life, there will be times we're going to "knee-jerk" with old ego, fearful habits and reactions. The niggles and larger feelings of disturbance signal those habitual fearful choices, and, simultaneously, the opportunities to choose again— to correct for peace. Growth toward peace and happiness requires this same choice for joining, again and again and again.

Summary of Key Ideas

- Focusing on what we don't want increases the energy of it.
- There is opportunity in every discomfort to align and become peaceful.
- Separating responses delay solution. Joining responses aid resolution.
- We all want to be connected, joined together in kindness, in peace.
- Asking to "see" differently guarantees a change of focus.
- We may trust that what we need to know will be given to us.

CHAPTER 11

Extending Love or Asking for It

Deep trust in life is not a feeling but a stance that you deliberately take! It's the attitude we call courage.

—Brother David Steindl-Rast

We're all physically here on planet Earth as actors in each other's dramas. In every interaction with another, we're either extending love or calling for it. And, they are doing the same. Once we become aware of this one drama that is always operating, we can easily discern what is occurring. We can then give/be the most appropriate response—Love. Either way—Love. The appropriate response will, of course, be to join or to answer the call—our own or another's. Either way, our response will be kind, loving, joining if we're consciously wanting peace.

That doesn't mean a sappy, condescending, surrendering response that ignores the importance of the situation. "Oh that's all right. Don't worry." The other person is clearly worried, upset, disturbed in some way and may feel we're responsible or just wants to complain. We're kind when we understand and join in loving support. We don't patronize. We openly hear the person, we acknowledge the feelings, the situation, and we stand by. We might say, "Whoa," or "Sounds pretty challenging," or "What are you thinking now?" Maybe, if you're truly willing, "Anything I can do?" If it's a stalled car and we have jumpers, offering a jump, a ride home, or waiting with them for the tow truck may be appropriate responses. To tell another person what they should do now, do it for them or take on the problem, in any way, isn't helpful. We're here to stand beside, not take over. Taking over is a demonstration of our superiority of knowing—all ego. We can share expertise or experience, but resist knowing what may be next for another. We don't have that kind of knowledge. The person with the problem is the person with the problem. It isn't ours to take on. We're there in a support role only. Just like parents, we don't help children when we make the bed for them. We stand by in encouragement, support, and perhaps helpfully instruct, as they figure it out.

Our ego fearful mind has become very habituated in responding to fear with more fear instead of love. We help ourselves when we come to bless the little niggle of disturbance and see it as the signpost that it is—an opportunity to again realign. In the process, we bless the other person who, unknowingly, served as the catalyst upon which we projected our thoughts. How else could we see who we currently think we are? Without the mirror of the "other," how could we notice the niggle of disturbance. This niggle always signals opportunity to change our minds, to choose again for love.

To be sure, there will be times when appropriate joining, truly helping, *is* our taking over—but only temporarily. Coming upon any situation where the other isn't able to decide the appropriate next action, we serve best with decisive action. That may be simply standing by, calling for help, applying first aid, and so on. In those situations, we truly help by, temporarily, choosing for them until they are capable to choose for themselves again.

We recognize help (love) is needed and give it, unselfishly. We want nothing In return.It's a call, though maybe nonverbal, for love and we answer with love. We give from love, not from ego superiority.

When we give from love, we don't assume the problem and become the savior of the situation. We offer able decision making until the owner of the problem is able to assume their own responsibility for choice. While it may momentarily look like taking over, it's really just standing by until the other is able to move forward with their own solutions. The person with the problem remains the person with the problem, we just help hold the space while they regain their ability to deal with it themselves. Again, our standing by, for however long we wish, never assumes the problem. It stands by in loving support only. We have probably all dealt with our ego selves in taking over situations under the false premise we're helping. Noticing our niggle of superiority will quickly move us back to helper, not savior! We trust the other with their own "problem" and the ability to resolve it. We're willing to brainstorm but not make the necessary choice of knowing how to proceed. We trust in the other person's ability to choose and our own courage to simply, supportingly, stand by.

Summary of Key Ideas

- Everything is either the extension of love or the call for it. Our response is the same either way—love.
- Love supports, allowing another their choice.
- Our ego nature would like to "fix." It enjoys the superiority of "knowing."
- We can't know what is best for another. They must choose for their own growth.
- The person with the problem, is the person with the problem.
- We can share ideas—if asked. Decisions are not ours.
- We may be required to temporarily decide if another is presently physically or emotionally incapable, and we step back when they are able again.

CHAPTER 12

Trusting the Help

Delegate to the manager. You have this really good staff that will take care of everything for you. You just have to delegate it and trust it.

—Abraham-Hicks

Genius is the ability to receive from the Universe.

—The I Ching

When you allow a full alignment with the Source within you, unpleasant things that may be happening around you will not matter. Instead of being influenced by the unwanted things that are happening, you will be influenced by your alignment with Source and with Well-being.

—Abraham-Hicks

As we have discussed earlier, what we have learned from our most ego educated ways, is that the only person you can really trust is yourself. There may be a kernel of wisdom in that idea, but most of us have probably had experiences with others that broadens that perspective. We may have had many interactions with trustworthy people in our lives, and known many trustworthy individuals. Humans, by the nature of being human, possess varying degrees of dependability and trustworthiness. We have all had different growth experiences that guide the way forward. It's my sincere belief that we're all doing the best we can in every moment. It doesn't make sense any other way. Is trustworthiness related to growth? Maybe.

Given the current perspective, the current experiential history, the current level of fear and the need to survive—in every present moment, given those parameters, we *always* make the best choice of which we're capable—right then. A nanosecond later, we or another may judge it as "not so good," but at the choice point, it was truly the best available choice to the one choosing. Why would we purposely make a bad choice? We don't. And in retrospect, we make lots of poor choices. That is the nature of the learning process. In learning what doesn't work, we find what does. Remember Thomas Edison and the lightbulb?

As we have realized earlier, fear plays a significant role in biasing the decision making process. The more disturbed and fearful way we're regarding the current situation, the more defensive our response may be, and the more we'll come from our ego in "knowing" what this means. Imagine we had an internal emotional meter, with a scale from one to ten. One is little fearful perspective, and ten is a majorly fearful perspective. The lower the level of perceived fear, the clearer our rational decision making can be. The higher the level of perceived fear, the less access we have to our rational mind for decision making. Disturbance above the hypothetical five is where we have less access to trust our own ability to decide wisely. Above five fear, flight or fight, takes over the decision making and our own best thinking is simply not available.

When we're willing to pay attention to the level of disturbance we experience, there are some strategies that may be helpful to reduce the irrational response and allow access to rational thought again. A deep breath is probably the quickest way to calm our fearful perspective and response. A deep breath creates a pause, a stopping of fear's escalation and that pause may be sufficient to access asking for help. From the space of a deep breath, we may recognize the futility of continuing to focus on the problem and move to asking for help with the solution. In contrast, fear would project us into ego knowing. The breath forestalls that knee-jerk ego arrogance, where what is best for everyone involved doesn't exist. Remember, this situation, by nature of it being some level of disturbance, is the call for love. Answering the call, joining in an appropriate way, changes the focus where we can move together toward solution.

Some years ago when traveling with my husband in the car, he said something, and I immediately withdrew into my defensive aloof, my preferred control drama for regaining perceived loss of power. Remember: control dramas are always manipulative and chief ego defenses. In this case, I perceived my being right was challenged and I could feel the urge to become knowingly withdrawn—defensively aloof. Because we had agreed to notice and work on our manipulative control dramas, with great risk, he said to me, "Honey, it looks like you're withdrawing into aloof."

Whoa! I noticed my urge to be further "not nice!" Instead, thankfully, I took a deep breath and was able to reply, "I hear that, thank you. I'm going to need a moment." I took another deep breath to emotionally distance myself from my erroneous perception, and mentally asked for help. Asking for help was a practiced part of my process at this point in my life, and has remained so. In a few minutes, I said him, "Thank you. I always want to be joined with you. Let's table this issue until we have a little more distance on it and are in a more neutral space." He readily agreed, and we joined hands. We easily, quickly dealt with the issue later that day. Being joined was always the most important focus, one which we both treasured. We knew, together, we could always find a mutual solution. Even if that solution was simply to agree to disagree for the time being.

Using the breath to stop an escalating ego drama is most helpful. It gives access to rationality, the place where we may choose again. We have simply made a habitual ego choice of perspective which served notice by our discomfort. The slippery slope is when we try to amend the situation on our own. It's interesting to note that the ego will always focus on the external resolution, which is only a representation of the real discord, always a nonphysical experiences of separation. Until we have grown to accept the importance of joining resolutions, power-with resolutions, we may retreat to old, habitual, ego-knowing, power-over resolutions. The deep breath creates the space to choose again. David Hawkins wrote an interesting book entitled *Power Vs Force* that wonderfully furthers the discussion of power-with versus power-over.

Obviously, willingness to choose again allows departing from ego choice and surrendering to Higher Knowing. Asking for help is really asking for guidance from the True Knowing. Trusting True Knowing is a growth process. "I would rather do it myself" is alive and well in each of us. That false ego confidence must be addressed in every life desiring peace and happiness. We're meant to align with Divine Knowing. It's a support system as easily given as the breath, which physically sustains us. It's always flowing, always available, but, unlike the breath, must be welcomed into awareness by asking. Free will, at its most expansive, is simply allowing the ever present guidance and support that is our birthright. Unless we remember, or ask, we don't become aware of what is already ours. Free will allows us to choose that support, or go it on our own, for as long as we wish. That choice is at the heart of this dualistic, planet Earth, life experience. The sooner we become aware of the choice for supportive alignment, the happier, and so much easier our life will be.

Our ego perceives we're on our own in this life experience. Our misperceptions about the supportive Source have been very prominent in our ignorance and unwillingness to access that always-available support. This Source has no religious affiliation, though some religious perspectives may understand It. There is no dogma to which one must adhere, and no particular perspective of "God," or even a "God," to which one must subscribe. It is, perhaps, described as a nameless, amorphous, nonjudgmental, indescribable, eternally present essence. Some call it God, Creator, Amma, Inner Wisdom, the Divine, Love— or innumerable other names. Looking for the broadest, most amorphous, uncharacterized term I can imagine, I simply call it Source Energy. To name it anything is a limitation, and we struggle with language here. You will find your way to what works for you. Finding your way to the trust of that life-giving support is crucial to true happiness. It's truly the Guide.

How will that guidance appear? My guess is there are probably as many ways as there are askers. It can be described as a knowing, an intuition, a nudge, or an awareness. Some see a meaningful sign; others hear something or just feel it. Things just take a turn from the previous ego perception. We're guided to move in a new direction that just feels more resolving and peaceful. Ellen Grace O'Brian said it well: "Divine guidance rarely offers mundane instruction about what to do. Instead, it comes as peace. It comes as love. It comes as truth. It comes as an invitation to abide in our essential wholeness and to let right action naturally unfold."

There is a noticeable letting go of what doesn't work and proceeding with what does. Balance is found again, ease comes back and we simply know a new way. Our asking is always answered, but we're never overridden. Asking invites Source Energy through our choice. Anything else would negate free will, the right to choose. When we ask, we're always answered— always. True asking leaves it all to Source Energy for direction. This asking isn't a list of what we want to make things right—that is supplication. True asking is simply sincere desire for helpful, joining change. It's ultimately asking for a change in perception from which new direction emerges. The miracle of *The Course in Miracles* is this shift in perception. It puts us back on track. We're realigned. We have, once again, assumed the responsibility for securing our own happiness. We're so powerfully endowed.

It's interesting to look at connections to Source Energy, Connecting Energy, with regard to its physical ramifications. Bruce Lipton wrote an interesting book called *The Biology of Perception*. He demonstrated the connection of "what we think" having an effect on each cell in the body. You can see where this is going. If we're aligned in our thinking, we support our own physical health. If we're misaligned, we're depleting the cells of our body from doing their amazing work of creating physical health and vitality. Obviously, this aligned perception scientifically adds to our being the powerful, happy individuals we wish most to be. We have the power to be peaceful in all circumstances—even in situations we would prefer not to have even occurred. It's all God. It's all for our experience of learning to choose. It's all perfect!

That seems pretty radical if we look back to the experience of the coronavirus. We want to argue that it was real, that it was something to truly fear. The ego always argues for its limiting physical perspectives. For some, seeing that situation from a place of resistance to the physical reality, played out in the living of that fear. Fear always creates more fear. We became hoarders, separated, closed off, as we feared for our very lives. There is no denial that we needed to make prudent choices for good health. But fearful panic took us beyond that sane, prudent response. Imagine if we had all simply made those prudent choices, stayed apart, and cared for each other respectfully. healthfully, and wisely. This was an opportunity to remember this. Some did and blessed us all. We're never on our own, but we can think we are if we care to do so. Happiness and peace reside in love, in joining, in alignment—in all circumstances. The nonphysical presides over the physical, not the other way around!

Summary of Key Ideas

- We're always doing the very best of which we're capable in every moment, even though a second later we may have a better choice.
- Fear distances us from rational thought. The more fear, the greater the distance.
- Feelings of discomfort indicate we're in a fearful perspective.
- A deep breath stops fear from escalating and helps to bring balance.
- Asking for help from True Knowing allows for a new perspective to enter into our awareness.
- True-knowing, Source Energy always answers.
- When Source Energy answers, we'll become aware of another way to see and interact with the situation, a way that allows us to become balanced, caring, and kind.

CHAPTER 13

It's All Relative!

Things are what they are. What they are to us is up to us.

—Ellen Grace O'Brian, *Daily Meditations*

Now, the world you see before you is in fact an out picturing of consciousness...

—The Guides, Alchemy, Paul Selig

Having "enough" is not an amount. It's a state of being.

—Lynne Twist

It's all relative. More accurate words are rarely spoken. And, we'll often fight arduously to deny those words. We earnestly believe our current perception of "reality" is the truth, is *real*. Few of us will readily admit it's simply *our* truth or a collective truth projected onto the situation or observation. All reality is projected reality. The observer affects the observed. Nothing comes into our awareness but through some method of observation, using our physical senses or our nonphysical knowing. Then, once we have observed, we attempt to understand what we have noticed. As with everything, we attempt to understand it using our own learning and experience as the basis for finding the meaning, or decoding what we encounter. Our own mind is the interpreter of the observation and then projects that deduced meaning onto the observed. We then believe that is the reality of it. Again, any meaning we have about anything comes from us. Then that meaning is projected onto the physical observation and believed to be its "reality." We do that individually and collectively. In either case, we rarely question the projected meaning and instead believe it to be the truth of the situation.

Using the example of a book, we can realize the collective meaning we take for granted about so many things. We have a common agreement as to the nature of a book. It's a collection of chapters, words, characters. It imparts information, stories, truths, imaginative ideas, collections of pictures, recipes, and so on. It can have a soft cover or a hard cover, an author or contributors, a colorful jacket or none. It could be a source of education, amusement, irritation, or material to be recycled. Our "knowledge" of the meaning of "book" increases as we grow depending on a books usefulness to us. For a college student, *book* may have a different meaning than to a belligerent teen, a toddler, or a member of a primitive illiterate family. To the scientist attempting to create a very lasting paper, it's a collection of findings about substances or experiments. So, we see that all meaning about the book is relative, even though it may be collectively agreed upon to be called a "book."

When we accept the nature of projected reality, we must also accept responsibility as the one projecting it! That realization is both daunting and powerfully exciting! We truly do create our own reality. Our projections are wonderful exhibits of the content of our own thoughts at any given moment. And our feelings let us know whether the thoughts we're projecting are enlivening, aligned with our nature as love, or are the depleting fearful thoughts of our ego nature. All projected thought is either life enhancing or life diminishing. It's actually a very incredible process and, if we're willing to recognize it, puts us completely in charge of our own happiness at all times. If the current perception doesn't feel good, and, therefore, isn't life enhancing, we can ask to see differently and get realigned. Simple but not necessarily easy. It isn't easy because we have such habitual confidence in external reality. There is no external reality! It's all projected! From a quantum physics perspective, we might think of the external world as just vibrating energy to which we have individually and collectively projected meaning! That is pretty mind blowing! I think we best leave the physics of reality and move back to the psychological dimension of it.

A Course in Miracles teaches that everything is opportunity. If we can open ourselves to this idea, it becomes a bit easier to accept the relative nature of everything. In every situation, we have the option to see an opportunity and not be trapped by a projected misperception that may currently feel very uncomfortable. Through discomfort, we come to know that there is always opportunity to see differently and become peaceful again. We want to argue that there are really "bad" circumstances for which this doesn't hold true. It's always true. Sometimes, in very difficult circumstances, it takes a while to accept our perceptual influence. We can all think of situations we have faced, that seemed so disastrous at the time, and later we saw as very helpful to our growth or understanding, even though we would have never invited or welcomed the situation.

At the extreme, death of a loved one is one such situation. Most probably there never would be a day we would have wanted that occurrence. But as we accepted it, we moved again to the peacefulness and understanding of the temporary nature of the physical, and the eternal nature of the soul. When we accept the nature of this earthly experience, we recognize physical death is an inevitability for us all. In that acceptance, we change the projected fearful perception of the situation, we see it differently, and move from an ego victim of the situation to an aligned calmness in a new perception of it. The happening of the physical situation doesn't change, but our experience of it does through the change in perception. This change is the opportunity to see differently that is *always* present through the willingness to ask. Source Energy always answers. We're forever supported by Source Energy.

Following the death of my husband, as you would suspect, I was devastated. There is no need to describe this; we have all experienced the death of a loved one. Having learned my perspective mattered, it occurred me that if I stayed in this black hole, I was going to be a very miserable woman for a long time. I sincerely asked for help, repeatedly. Eventually, I allowed that help into my awareness. The idea to spend some time in gratitude came to me. For the next year, I reminisced about the wonderful life we had had together. In the car, I listened to our high school and college music. With the help of my oldest daughter, we sorted old photos. After she left each of these many sessions, I went back and gathered the most meaningful photos. These, I secretly saved in a digital collection to be used as a photo book to give each of the children the following Christmas, to which I added poems I had written to and about him, and other commentary. We all treasure that wonderful book full of memories of Dad. I still look at it joyfully and gratefully. I can truthfully say, I haven't had a sorrowful moment since. Joy and gratitude fill every photo, with thoughts of him and memories our life together.

We never know, in physical form, how Source Energy will respond to our asking. We absolutely know, we'll be answered! What an incredible assurance.

Summary of Key Ideas

- There is no intrinsic reality, there is only relative reality as observed reality.
- The observer affects the observed.
- We project meaning onto everything we observe.
- Feelings allow us to know if our projections are enlivening or depleting.
- Willingness to allow a shift in perception, through asking for help, returns us to balance and peace.

CHAPTER 14

Gratitude

Grateful living generates sustainable, resilient well-being in our lives, and it's how we can best care for the planet and one another—grounded in love and gratitude.

—Kristi Nelson

If the only prayer you ever say in your entire life is thank you, it will be enough.

— Meister Eckhart

Appreciation is the highest form of prayer, for it acknowledges the presence of good wherever you shine the light of your thankful thoughts.

—Alan Cohen

Even though we may understand the relative nature of perception, again and again, we find ourselves caught in old habitual patterns, the patterns where we give unalterable false reality to externals. These patterns are passed along in families and cultures. Until we're willing to recognize discomfort, as the alert to a perception that doesn't serve us, we'll continue to believe what we have always believed—whether it serves our happiness or not. The collective nature of our perceptions is our current belief system, our BS! Whatever perceptions we currently hold, stories we're telling ourselves, comprises our outlook and our belief system.

The other euphemism often associated with that acronym is very telling when our belief system isn't creating happiness and isn't enlivening.

Discomfort, unhappiness, and upset are the clues that we're projecting perceptions that are not serving our happiness. How blessed we are to have such a marvelous early warning system already built in! But it's only an effective notification when we pay attention to it! Noticing discomfort, as the indication of misperception, allows us to take responsibility, ask for help, and return to comfort as soon as possible. Ignoring the discomfort and continuing to believe misperceptions, leads us to the slippery slope of victim posturing. The road back to happiness requires much more work and backtracking from a victim position. Remember: from the position of a misguided victim posture, the ego is in full reign and will staunchly stand ground in its perceived "rightness." In this justification, it will reject help or any loosening of its stance.

So obviously, the earlier we're willing to notice the uncomfortable feelings that always signify misperception, the quicker we can get back on track and feel good again. The challenge here is to avoid the ego's self-serving physical solutions. They never lead to peace. This is the time to ask the Supporting Energy, Inner Wisdom, Source, for help. It's time to ask to see differently, to ask to be shown the way. The ego never wants to give up selfish control, so our surrendering to something greater won't be its choice. It's time for courage and determined desire. To return to peace, we must surrender to the process that ensures it— asking for help from Sustaining Energy.

> *Courage is not the absence of fear, but rather the judgment that something else is more important than one's fear.*
>
> —Ambrose Hollingworth Redmoon

To the ego, the word *surrender* means giving up. It means being powerless. The surrender to Source Energy is, actually, just the opposite. It's only discomfort and unhappiness that we're giving up. It's giving up what isn't serving us. Perhaps it's more palatable if we speak of it as giving over. Giving over, what isn't serving our happiness, to make room for what will serve us. It's releasing the ego's hold, of attempting to control the externals, to Spirit's guidance to regain internal stability, peace and happiness.

Though perhaps redundant, it's important to remember, the ego holds tightly to the misperceptions causing discomfort, the unhappy feelings, because the fear is useful. The ego is *always* motivated by fear, fear of being unable to control the externals. Since we can never control the externals, though it may appear so temporarily, the ego can never achieve its goal. We've lost the choice for happiness under any ego direction. Short term "winning" isn't possible to sustain because the ego always wins at the expense of others. The ego must be top dog, therefore, someone else must be "less than"—lower dog. This can never feel good, whether acknowledged or not, guilt always underlies ego decision making. Guilty feelings are not comfortable and never lead to happiness.

There are two amazing shortcuts to help create the path out of discomfort. Of course, we must first pay attention to the discomfort, which signals the need for change. As we have mentioned earlier, the breath is the first arbitrator for peace. As soon as we detect our uncomfortable feelings, taking a very deep breath creates a space that interrupts the process and stops it from escalating. The deep breath settles down our discomfiting emotions and creates a space where we might return to rational choice. It stops the ego storytelling in its tracks.

The second shortcut, even though we initially doubt its usefulness, is gratitude. We initially reject the idea of gratitude because we think it has to be about the situation at hand. It doesn't. Gratitude about anything is the most immediate, direct path out of ego perception. The ego is never grateful because it never has enough. Gratitude about anything is having enough in this tiny moment. This gratitude doesn't have to be related to the current situation in any way. It can be about the bird that we hear singing, it can be about the comfort of the seat we occupy, it can be about the wonderful dinner we're considering. Any gratitude recognized will turn the tide of upset to the peace of appreciation. It reestablishes emotional balance so we may proceed from a more rational perspective. Said another way, it moves us from ego control to Love's guidance.

Sam Keen makes the point well: "...the more you become a connoisseur of gratitude, the less you are victim of resentment, depression, and despair. Gratitude will act as an elixir that will gradually dissolve the hard shell of your ego—your need to possess and control—and transform you into a generous being. The sense of gratitude produces true spiritual alchemy, makes us magnanimous—large souled."

Gratitude is so easy to employ. We simply have to remember to employ it. Gratitude is the quickest ticket out of the ego's mis-perceptive nature. We take a breathing pause and ponder what we have, rather than continuing to focus on what we don't have. When sitting in gratitude, no matter how briefly, we're aligned with our true nature. Thus, we're automatically more peaceful.

For most of us, it takes practice not to jump back into discomforting thoughts. When we do jump back, we just take another deep breath and realign. We always have the choice to realign. Gratitude is an immediate aid—and so easy!

Summary of Key Ideas

- A collection of perceptions constitute our belief system, our BS.

- When we're uncomfortable, our belief system isn't serving us.

- A deep breath interrupts growing a depleting belief system.

- Moving to gratitude, about anything, immediately moves us from depleting perceptions to enlivening perceptions.

- Surrendering isn't giving up—it's giving over.

- Surrendering misperception to Higher Guidance allows for change.

- Gratitude moves us from ego guidance to Love's Guidance.

CHAPTER 15

Energetic Alignment

There are no guarantees.
From the viewpoint of fear none are strong enough.
From the viewpoint of love none are necessary.

—Emmanuel

The reason you want every single thing that you want, is because you think you will feel really good when you get there. But, if you don't feel really good on your way to there, you can't get there. You have to be satisfied with what-is while you're reaching for more.

—Abraham-Hicks

The only way for anyone to be consistently happy is to understand that the feeling happiness is simply about alignment with the Source within.

—Abraham-Hicks

We have been talking about gratitude as a way to quickly switch from a negative, energy depleting perspective to a positive, enlivening perspective. Gratitude changes the energy of negative perception and stops us on the path to greater discomfort. It creates an energetic change of direction that now facilitates peace instead of distracting from it.

At the center of everything, including us, is an energetic vibration. How we manage that vibration is the choice we have been examining in various ways. Our vibrational energy is either sustaining us or depleting us. Those are the only two choices. Most of us haven't been consciously aware of this choice and our part in maintaining it. It really is a very critical choice. Perhaps it's the most critical choice!

We might look at this choice as the fuel of our lives. Positive energy, or vibration, propels us forward into growth on so many levels. Negative energy creates a stall and a depletion of life energy, the extent of which depends upon its strength and duration. Logically, we would only want positive energy, a positive energy vibration. Many of us live from predominantly negative perspectives and, consequently, what we perceive as negative lifestyles. We don't have to continue to do so. But we must take responsibility for managing our energetic vibration. While this may seem like an insurmountable task, it's really quite uncomplicated. We simply dedicate ourselves to paying attention to how we feel, one feeling at a time. That **is** our energy vibration!

Feelings are the indicator of our vibrational perspective in any moment. That perspective is created by our projected perception about what we think is occurring—the story we're telling. If it doesn't feel good, a change of perception is required. We have supplied the perception, as described earlier, and we have the power to initiate the change of perception. When needed, our job is to ask for the change of perception but not to supply it. The asking is our role, the supply comes from Universal Mind, Source Energy.

If we rely upon ourselves, the small self, to supply the change of perception, we're drawing from the same well that created it. It's how we arrived at the negative perception, and consequent discomforting feelings, in the first place. Now is the time to go big! We go to Source Energy because that energy is always positive, always enlivening. Our discomforting feeling served as the misalignment signal and now we're wanting to consciously realign with the vibration that is life sustaining and propelling. We actually have never been disconnected; we have just temporarily blocked or distracted ourselves from its ever-flowing supply. We do have free will, we can choose to be aligned or go it on our own at every juncture. This is the essence of the journey in each physical experience here. Now is the time for us to remove the block and allow the supply an easy flow again.

This is the constant process of every life in this dualistic earthly experience. To one degree or another, we all have habitually practiced the choices that don't lead to happiness. As we're blessed to recognize our role in these choices, we empower ourselves to choose again, repeatedly. This is the practice of each life that desires to take responsibility for their own happiness. It's a simple process, but not an easy one initially. It requires dedication to the task of changing old habits. It's absolutely possible, one feeling, one choice at a time.

We're the powerful choosers. Now is the time for action. Results are guaranteed.

The Universal Mind, Source Energy, is ever sustaining, ever flowing. The decision of whether to "hook-up" is always ours at every juncture of discomfort and conscious recognition. We grow into accepting the responsibility of choice that happiness requires. Old fearful, ego, separating habits die hard. Accepting ourselves as the "choice creators" of discomfort is difficult to acknowledge. Intellectually, we may see it, but still not accept it. It takes dedication to notice feelings every time! It's much easier to just let someone else be "the reason why."

It's important to realize blame has no part in a supportive choice. Blame is a projection of responsibility. We blame others, victimize, so we don't have to take responsibility. We blame ourselves for the same reason. It's "the devil made me do it," mentality. Blame is useless, a distraction from the path forward. See it when it comes up, spend no time wallowing, and move on to a more enlivening choice. To stop and beat ourselves up for an old habit is a stall, and useless. It's much more useful to celebrate our recognition of what doesn't work, and move on to the choice for what does. This is the process of growth. Let's hold as few pity parties as possible. Let's engage with our process of change eagerly! Remember, everything is opportunity.

Again, it's an energetic universe, at its most basic, and simultaneously at its most complex. Isn't that an interesting dichotomy? We're composed of that same complexity. Our power lies in the recognition and utilization of that complexity, the choice to align one necessity, one misperception at a time. Each signaling discomfort exposes a depleting choice, and, at the same time, gifts us with the opportunity to choose again.

What an amazing abundance we have been given with the endowment of free will. Through the gift of choice, we may energetically realign at will. Willingness is the key to allowing realignment with peace, with happiness. Ask and it's given. Every time.

Summary of Key Ideas

- Gratitude immediately shifts the energy, the vibration, from negative to positive.
- We're the powerful managers of our energy through the perceptions that we choose.
- Positive energy propels us forward—negative energy stalls our progress.
- When we recognize a change of energy is needed (notice discomfort), it's time to ask to see differently.
- Trying to see differently, is reemploying the ego—not truly asking.
- Supporting Source Energy always answers.

CHAPTER 16

Opportunity, Even in Chaos?

Focusing on what we don't want, instead of what we want ... no happiness there.

Worrying is using your imagination to create something you don't want.

—Abraham-Hicks

In everything, there is always opportunity. That opportunity, of course, plays out from our thoughts about the situation. The opportunity is in choosing how we think about and project onto the situation. Therefore, the recent experience generated by the coronavirus must have been pregnant with opportunity also. What were/are the opportunities collectively and individually for us? That's the question, isn't it. That is always the question. Are we willing to explore the possibilities or will we stay focused on the catalyst instead?

Maybe a little of both? Awareness of the physical situation seems important and responding with prudence can be wise. Is it prudent to engage our awareness in thoughtful, calm, peaceful ways? Sometimes, we respond with alarm, insecurity and great fear. We're the choosers of our own thought path. And, those choices create our experience, both physically and energetically. What is our gift to others, and to ourselves, in chaotic times? Peace generates more peace. Fear generates more fear. We're powerful choosers with every thought and every response.

In all chaos, while being prudent with intelligent action, it would seem enlivening, supportive, and en-heartening to explore our own and the collective opportunities. There is much more peace in investigating possibilities than there is in dire, fearful prognostication. Chaos is a time to find the opportunities to support well-being, to enliven ourselves!

There is always much information coming toward us. With all of it, we have to decide what has personal value and usefulness. All information is opinion and perspective, on very fluctuating "realities." Granted some information seems supported by intelligence and goodwill. Some of it will fall into the category of sensationalism or manipulation. We each have to sort that out and take what is useful and supports well-being for us. A good filter might be: Is it of benefit for me, and, at the same time, is it of benefit for all? Supporting the greater good ultimately does support the individual.

Remember: the useful measuring stick for determining the supporting/not-supporting nature of information is how it feels. Feelings are indicators of that which enlivens us and that which doesn't. Feelings that generate peace, ease, and contentment support life. As said earlier, every cell in our bodies responds to the thoughts we're having. The value of the thoughts we're having is indicated by how we feel. Pretty simple: Feeling good, supports thriving. Feeling discomfort doesn't. Who generates the thoughts or perceptions about anything? We do! We're powerful choosers and it behooves us to pay attention to thought choices and their ramifications. Peter McWilliams said, "You can't afford the luxury of a negative thought." That's it! Our awareness of choice is what allows us to create lives supporting well-being and, ultimately our happiness.

So what are the opportunities in chaos? The same as with all of life, the chaos puts choice before us. The results of our choices and the delicacy of life is in our awareness at a heightened level. What if floods, fires, melting ice caps, earthquakes, tornadoes, and hurricanes are also opportunities to notice imbalance and lack of care for our home, the earth and each other? Famine, violence, disease allow us to notice opportunities to care for our brothers and sisters and ultimately for ourselves. Maybe these events hold up the mirror for noticing needed change. In chaos there is heightened awareness of the opportunity—for kindness, for compassionate care, for joining together to come through.

We must keep before us what we truly desire—peace and well-being. We must make the choices that facilitate the fulfillment of those desires. Perhaps it's time to become more consciously involved in caring for and loving each other and our home. We're the powerful choosers, let's choose again. Let's notice the opportunities before us to join together to create a world that is cared for, and a human family focused on compassion and kindness. We've failed to notice where we were going, but now we're awake! We're in this life expression together, and we'll come through change together also. Now is the time to remember we're one humanity with a live and vibrant home. Let's commit anew to it's care and our caring.

Summary of Key Ideas

- Everything is the same opportunity to choose our lens of perception: ego or Aligned Mind.
- Every situation allows that same choice of observation.
- We're the choosers of our peace through the choice of our perceptual lens.
- When we aren't peaceful and happy, we have chosen erroneously.
- We may always choose again.
- Every choice leads somewhere.
- Being clear about what we want for ourselves, our brothers and sisters and the planet guides our choices.

CHAPTER 17

Allowing Happiness

The habit of being happy enables one to be freed, or largely freed, from domination of outward conditions.

—Robert Louis Stevenson

The standard of success in life isn't the things. It isn't the money or the stuff—it is absolutely the amount of joy you feel.

—Abraham-Hicks

What is happiness? What is it that pushes us forward every moment? What is it that we want most in life? It all seems to come down to happiness, that feeling that in this nanosecond, all is well. It's a satisfaction, a peacefulness and joy that is deeply comforting and enriching. Though often we find it temporary or fleeting, especially when we have tied it to something external to us, it can be a more fully, lasting experience than most of us realize.

Happiness is an inside job. Lasting happiness is a result of the willingness to understand the connection between perception, projection and feelings. Then, to have the willingness to seek help when we need it. This simple formula guarantees the results we desire, and is rarely sustainably practiced. Instead, we routinely practice old habits, based in ego fear, that cannot produce the happiness for which we yearn. Understanding our misguided ways and courageously creating new habits that serve our happiness, are the keys to the change we want. It seems daunting but actually it can be quite possible, easy, and exhilarating when we look at it as a one-thought-at-a-time project. We build a new internal programming by asking for the shift of one misperception at a time. Just one. The little satisfaction that comes with amending one misperception is very motivating and leads to doing it again! The success with that one, leads to repeating the process with the next one and it builds change in habit. We can all do that.

Creating real change in our lives isn't a light-switch operation. We don't say, "That's it! I'm not doing that anymore. I'm going to do only this now!" For most of us, old habits are more tenacious than to succumb to simple determinations, though occasionally that is possible. Usually, we have to use our determination, for noticing the error in perception, in order to be able to address it, as that is the only time the need for change is evident! Uncomfortable feelings are the "notifier." They are the catalyst indicating a needed change of perception. That is a good thing, and the reason why everything is opportunity! "If it ain't broke, don't fix it." And, logically, if it's broken—do fix it! A problem, a collection of repeated misperceptions, is the catalyst for change, if seen as opportunity. The most expedient and satisfying path is to accept the notification, and get on with finding a solution. Resistance and complaining about the problem simply delays the process of resolution and delays our return to balance and happiness.

What we're talking about is a new perception of misperception! A new perception of discomfort. When we learn to recognize it as a signal for change, an opportunity for movement back to happiness, we become more accepting of the temporary discomfort, and perhaps, more quickly see it as useful! It's the signal that we have choices to make, choices that will lead us back to what we always want—balance and happiness. Happiness is an inside job. Only we can recognize when it isn't present, only we can take responsibility for the misperception that produces it, and only we can be willing to choose to see differently! That ability to choose is the magnificent free will with which we're all inherently gifted. Our wonderful ability to choose is what provides us all with the key to our own happiness. Once understanding this, it seems only reasonable that we would want to step up and create our own happiness. And do it as often as necessary to establish the habit of happiness that is the harbinger of a truly successful life experience. We're meant to be joyous and have been provided with all the tools necessary to accomplish it.

We're the "allowers" of our own happiness. We're the determined builders of the life we truly desire. We're the powerfully endowed creators of our own happiness. What an amazing, exhilarating, exciting, encouraging realization. And, it has been ours for the recognizing all along. Knowing this, victim options will never be as enticing. We'll now more quickly step into the powerful truth of ourselves and welcome the signaling opportunities to rebalance—to choose again. We can do it and do it excitedly. It's the most amazing, exhilarating, rewarding realization, and available to every one of us! The magnificent gift of free will is always ours! We're all endowed with it. We can always choose again, choose to have perception aligned, and know happiness again in each moment. Through the endowed gift of free will we're incredibly powerful beings.

Summary of Key Ideas

- We all want to be happy.
- Happiness is an inside job, we're the determiners of our own happiness.
- We tell the story of everything we observe (our perception) and then experience feelings about the story we told.
- We have habitually believed that those things observed external to us are real.
- They are only a perceptual reality created by us. We're the storytellers.
- Feelings tell us whether our current story (perception) is enlivening or depleting.
- We feel happy with enlivening perceptions, uncomfortable, dis-eased with depleting perspectives.
- We must observe and take responsibility for every perception we hold. We must notice the signal of discomfort and be willing to amend those that don't serve us.
- Noticing a need for a changed perspective is a lifetime practice.
- Free will is the opportunity to choose (allow happiness) again, and again, and again.

CHAPTER 18

Who, Whose Am I?

So, the rule of thumb has to be: "I'm going to be very, very, very happy, and then do everything I have time to do after that."

—Abraham-Hicks

Our mandate in life is to become all that we can be. That becoming is ultimately not for ourselves but for the common good and for life itself.

—Gunilla Norris

We all have a creation story, the story about how we got here in the first place. There are probably as many stories as there are people. Those stories could be arranged in categories, evolution stories, biblical stories, biological stories, quantum physics stories, and so on. We each have to figure out our own story, and, for those of us who are parents, probably had to think of one that we could responsibly share. As we have grown and matured, physically and spiritually, our stories have probably endured a great deal of change. For most of us, the big questions of life are approached from more depth and experience as we mature and we modify them accordingly.

The big questions of "Who Am I?' "What Am I?' "Why Am I?" are pondered by most of us at some level. We seek to have an understanding of the reason for life, the meaning of our life. My first recollection of these questions began around the age of twelve. They were unsettling, often fearful thoughts at that age. They were focused on a physical perspective of trying to think of what was the earth, what was the universe, what was beyond the universe, what was beyond the void, beyond, beyond, beyond?

And, what happened to us after we die? Where/what was heaven? Was there heaven? These were very terrifying thoughts because they didn't have any satisfactory answers. There was no peace in the not-knowing. They remained unsettling for many years and I would purposely avoid thinking about these questions. Even so, they would occasionally, frighteningly creep back in.

Newly married, settling into sleep for the night, my thoughts somehow drifted back into the disturbing quandary of those unanswerable questions and I startled myself, and my dear sleeping husband, by suddenly shouting, "Get me Oreos! Get me Oreos!"

Having already drifted off, he woke with, "What? Whhaaat?"

I repeated with urgency, "Get me Oreos? Now! Just get me Oreos!"

Often perplexed by me but deeply loving, he hopped up from bed, stumbled out to the kitchen and quickly returned with the Oreos, which I rapidly began chomping. More grounded, I began to settle, before his very curious, watchful eyes.

"What the h—— was that?" he asked, bewildered.

I had to then confess my "what-was-beyond" fearful questioning.

He, of course, said, "Well, just don't think about it."

"Easier said than done," I replied. Another account to his ever-accumulating experience of my "weirdness," of which he often lovingly reminded me.

My response always was, "Well, you picked me." He would then sweetly, smugly chuckle.

Over the years, the questioning moved from less about the physical dynamics to more about the nonphysical, spiritual questions of existence. Years and years of reading, studying, conferences and spiritual experiences has allowed me to settle into a place that both puts my questioning at rest and allows me a great peace. Like everyone else, we're never going to get mutually agreeable answers to those questions, but we can figure out what works for us. Where I settled was in alignment with Wayne Dyer's statement, "I'm a spiritual being having a physical experience," and understanding that it isn't the other way around! That idea of the truth of us as spiritual beings allowed the ground to settle in place for me.

What if we're beings of love, created by Love, spiritual beings? Love, the ever expanding "Isness." Love, whose only characteristic is to be more, to expand. Love, the joining element of all, the foundational energy of happiness. In the energy of love, all is well. Peace abides and happiness is. While romantic love can certainly be a representation of this love, it's that and also more than that at the same time. A word often used is agape. Agape love might be described as brotherly love or love for all of creation. There is no "ego" deserving, no qualifiers with agape love. It's the basis of who we are and how we most richly join with all of life, which is equally created and endowed by love. We're all in the process of recognizing and realizing that joining, agape connection. Every event of our lives is that same opportunity to recognize the truth of ourselves, and all others, as equally created, equally on the path of discovering our Truth. We're one—One.

We're indeed One, and life is a process for remembering this Truth. It's this continuous discovery for which the physical experience serves as the vehicle. It's why everything is opportunity. It's the opportunity to experience our truth, to choose joining, to align with agape love, Source Energy, again and again and again until it's realized as Us.

It is, of course, possible to sit in this awareness in all circumstances. For most of us, it takes practice in remembering. It takes practice in stepping away from our ego habit and choosing again, choosing to repeatedly live from that place of joining, well-being, peace. We might, again, liken the choice as one of perceptual reference. We can choose to be an actor on the stage of the current life drama or a witness of the drama from a seat in the audience. The observed or the observer. The absorbed participant or the witness. That choice is presented in every situation, every opportunity, every experience of life. That perceptual choice alone creates what follows in our experience. Our lives are created, experience by experience, from that same choice repeated. It's the vehicle for recognizing the Truth of ourselves, the Truth of us all, the Truth of our Oneness.

We're Love, created by Love. Those are the simplest and most expansive, most satisfying words to describe our existence. That perspective offers a glorious place from which to exist, from which to expand, and from which to be. We're human beings— not human "doings." Remembering our truth as spiritual beings, brings our life focus to one focus, one task, one path. When we know who we are and whose we are, we're supported by the Is-ness of All. We constantly allow that Is-ness into our experience by remembering it and asking for it when we're again in the forgetful "pickle." The answering is guaranteed. Guaranteed! It's built in, part of us, only Us!

We can be happy! We can choose alignment, peace and ease at every opportunity. Life is only this joyous choice/opportunity to remember again and again until we are it! We're all here to practice that choice. It's the repeated choice to remember Who and Whose we are. And, we practice, we do it until we are It!! This is the purpose of life—to be who we are, to be joyous, to be happy!

We're Love and loved. Life is about this realization. We're the divine of the Divine. Be who you are!! Allowing alignment with our Truth is being happy. We're the allowers of happiness. We're what we seek.

Joyous ride!

REFERENCES

Anonymous. 1975. *A Course in Miracles*. Tiburon: Foundation for Inner Peace.

Barks, Coleman, with John Moynhe, translators. 1995. *The Essential Rumi*. San Francisco: Harper Collins.

Godman, David. 1985. *The Teachings of Sri Ramana Maharshi*. New York: Penguin Group.

Gunther, Bernard. 1979. *Dying for Enlightenment, Living with Bhagwan Shree Rajneesh (Osho)*. New York: Harper and Row.

Noris, Gunilla. 2017. *Embracing The Seasons: Memories of a Country Garden*. New York: BlueBridge.

Redfield, James. 1993. *The Celestine Prophecy*. New York: Warner Books.

Ryce, Michael. 1966. *Why Is This Happening to Me Again*. Dr. Michael Ryce.

Selig, Paul. 2020. *Alchemy*. New York: St.Martin's Publishing.

Selig, Paul. 2019. *Beyond the Known, Realization*. New York: St. Martin's Publishing.

Miller, Carolyn. 1995. *Creating Miracles*. Tiburon: H. J. Kramer.

Mitchell, Stephen, translator. 1988. *Tao Te Ching, a new English version*. New York: Harper & Row.

Walker, Brian Browne, translator. 1992. *The I Ching*. New York: St. Martin's Griffin.